GOURMET
SANDWICHES

NORMAN KOLPAS

D1370498

HPBooks

a division of

PRICE STERN SLOAN

Los Angeles

Cover photo and food styling by Burke/Triolo Photography

Illustrations by Michelle Burchard

Published by HPBooks
a division of Price Stern Sloan, Inc.
11150 Olympic Boulevard
Los Angeles, California 90064
©1993 Norman Kolpas
Illustrations © 1993 Price Stern Sloan, Inc.

Library of Congress Cataloging-in-Publication Data

Kolpas, Norman.
    Gourmet sandwiches / by Norman Kolpas.
        p.   cm.
    Includes index.
    ISBN 1-55788-043-3
    1. Sandwiches.   I. Title.
TX818.K65   1993
641.8'4—dc20   92-44838
                                                          CIP

Printed in the United States of America

10 9 8 7 6 5 4 3 2 1

NOTICE: The information in this book is true and complete to the best of our knowledge. All recommendations are made without any guarantees on the part of the author or Price Stern Sloan. The author and publisher disclaim all liability in connection with the use of this information.

This book is printed on acid-free paper.

Acknowledgments

Friends and family too numerous to list here have been witting and unwitting subjects to my sandwich testing over the years; thank you all. But acknowledgment for their roles as the ultimate accomplices to the happy madness of eating a meal between two slices of bread goes to my wife and son, Katie and Jacob Kolpas, who make every meal fun.

My special thanks go to the many chefs and restaurant owners who generously contributed their own outstanding sandwich recipes, which appear throughout this book and include individual acknowledgments. They all deserve special credit for helping to change the public's perception of the once-humble sandwich.

Everyone at HPBooks receives my sincerest appreciation for all their support and encouragement.

Contents

Introduction

Look at any trend-setting restaurant today and you'll find strong evidence that the humble sandwich is suddenly more popular—more delightfully varied—than ever before.

It's served on incredibly flavorful—sometimes even unusual—fresh-baked bread. It includes a rich, wondrous, often elegant—and sometimes surprising—assortment of fillings. It's sauced and garnished to delightful effect.

To be sure, the sandwich is still, as always, convenient food—an easily assembled meal in itself. And it's comfort food—the perfect traditional-style repast for an era that sees a return to home-based values.

But the modern sandwich also reflects the present day's more highly developed culinary sensibility. It displays the influences of many different cuisines: Asian, Middle Eastern, European and Latin American. It sparkles with the fresher, more varied ingredients that sophisticated cooks and diners now expect as their due.

This book chronicles the delightful new world of sandwiches. It begins with a brief guide to all the many different sandwich components, from breads to fillings, sauces and condiments to garnishes. This introductory section is followed by four recipe chapters organized by filling type: Meats, Poultry, Seafood and Dairy & Vegetables.

Scattered throughout the chapters, you'll also find contributions from some of America's most innovative chefs—proof positive that the humble sandwich has attained an elevated culinary status indeed.

No matter how exalted the sandwich may have become, however, all these recipes have one important characteristic in common with the sandwiches of yore: They are easy to prepare, producing delightful results with minimal effort. And that rare combination of ease and satisfaction is, in the end, central to the sandwich's enduring appeal.

A Guide to Sandwich Ingredients

Almost everyone knows that the sandwich is a relatively recent invention—the late-18th-century brainchild of John Montagu, Britain's fourth earl of Sandwich, who recognized the casual convenience and neatness of layering a slice of meat between two slices of bread. How amused his lordship might be to observe the imaginative elaborations wrought upon his simple little concept!

Breads

"White, wheat or rye?" is a refrain familiar to the ears of anyone who has ever ordered a sandwich in a coffee shop or diner. For the most part, I've restricted the bread suggestion for each recipe to these few basics along with other readily available breads such as sourdough, pumpernickel and multi-grain breads—along with now-common pita breads (Middle Eastern-style pocket breads), French baguettes, assorted rolls and croissants.

But part of the joy of sandwiches today is the amazing and ever-growing choice of breads that may now be purchased in cities and small towns alike. Enterprising commercial bakers and small boutique bakeries are offering breads scented with rosemary, dill, mustard, fennel seed or other heady seasonings; breads studded with caramelized onions, briny ripe olives or sweet-tart sun-dried tomatoes; breads enriched with cornmeal, millet, brown rice, oat bran or other unusual and healthful grains. In short, breads of imagination-boggling variety are now available.

I wholeheartedly suggest that you seek out new, high-quality bakeries in your own community. Try their breads. Bring a new loaf home, try a slice, then leaf through this book and find a recipe that sounds suited to it. Don't restrict yourself to the choices I've given here. Let your imagination and your taste buds run wild.

To toast or not to toast: Toasting bread for a sandwich serves two main purposes. From a practical standpoint, it helps keep the bread crisp, preventing the sandwich from getting soggy and falling apart as you eat it—as well as providing a coarser surface to "grip" the filling and keep the sandwich together. Aesthetically, toasting gives the bread a different flavor and texture that may in some cases better complement the qualities of the filling. I've borne both these aspects in mind

when deciding whether or not to toast the bread in each particular recipe, but if your own tastes lean in a direction opposite the one that I have taken, feel free to follow your own preference.

Fillings

To state the obvious, sandwich fillings may be classified into the main categories that comprise the chapters of this book: Meats, Poultry, Seafood and Dairy & Vegetables. But the particular appeal of the modern sandwich derives in good part from the many ways in which these elements may be combined—cheeses, for example, highlighting particular meats, or grilled or marinated vegetables enhancing various poultry or seafood fillings. By selecting two or more complementary ingredients to fill a sandwich, you set up the dynamic interplays of taste, texture and color that feature in fine cooking.

Roasting peppers: Roasting develops and enhances the flavor of bell peppers and gives them a pleasing tenderness—qualities that complement any sandwich in which they are included.

Place the whole peppers in a shallow baking dish or on a baking sheet with a rim and place in a 400°F (205°C) oven. When the skins blacken and blister on top, turn the peppers and continue roasting until they are evenly blackened, 20 to 30 minutes.

Remove peppers from oven and cover loosely with a kitchen towel until cool enough to handle. Then peel off blistered skins and pull off stems. Finally, remove seeds and ribs from inside, using a teaspoon if necessary to pick up stray seeds.

This same method may also be applied to fresh hot chile peppers. Bear in mind when handling such peppers, however, that they contain oils that can cause a painful burning sensation upon contact with the eyes or skin. Use kitchen gloves to protect your hands if you have cuts or abrasions, or if your skin is sensitive. Wash your hands liberally with plenty of warm, soapy water after handling the chiles. Take special care not to touch your eyes after handling chiles. If you do so accidentally, splash plenty of cool water into your eyes to rinse them.

Toasting nuts: Toasted nuts have a rich flavor and crunchy texture that may be used to enhance a sandwich filling.

To toast nuts, spread them in a single layer on a shallow baking sheet and place in a 325°F (160°C) oven. When nuts are light golden in color, 8 to 12 minutes depending on variety and size, remove from oven and let cool before using; they will continue to darken slightly from their residual heat.

Condiments

The wide range of condiments—mayonnaises, mustards, ketchups, chutneys and the like— serve both to flavor a sandwich and to moisten it.

That latter role is often sadly overlooked, particularly when sandwiches are made with leftover ingredients that have lost some of their natural moisture. A good slathering of mayonnaise goes a long way to restore appealing moisture to a sandwich filling.

Good-quality mayonnaise is readily available in supermarkets, and everyone seems to have his or her favorite brand. For the purpose of sandwich-making, I find such products just as good as homemade mayonnaise—particularly when you consider the time involved in making the latter.

But let those who gain an air of culinary superiority by making their own go ahead and do so!

One final important point about mayonnaise must be addressed here: its fat content. An emulsion of egg yolks and oil, mayonnaise is high in fat, cholesterol and calories. But those of us who are watching what we eat need no longer worry on that account: Commercial brands of lowfat and even fat-free mayonnaise are now being sold in supermarkets and provide—to my health-conscious taste, at least—much of the same luscious quality as their more sinful counterparts.

Garnishes & Accompaniments

Whether a simple dill pickle, a pile of French fries or an elaborate pasta salad devised since the Earl of Sandwich's time to accompany sandwiches—so many accompaniments and garnishes, in fact, that they would more than merit a book unto themselves. When selecting a garnish or accompaniment—whether from the supermarket shelf, the local deli case or your own repertoire of recipes—bear in mind that the object is to complement the sandwich rather than overshadow it. Keep accompaniments simple, and the sandwich will remain the star.

Remember, too, that sandwiches—even some of the more elaborate creations on the pages that follow—are meant to be simple to prepare and eat; so don't take on too much more work than the sandwich itself. Better to tear open a bag of imaginatively seasoned potato chips than to fry up a batch yourself!

The Earl of Sandwich—who, after all, created the sandwich with ease, neatness and simplicity in mind—would no doubt have approved.

Meat Sandwiches

Ask most people to describe their favorite sandwich, and more likely than not you'll hear meat mentioned—so inextricably linked are the concepts of sandwiches and hearty eating.

To be sure, you'll find hearty recipes here—bread piled high with sliced beef, crisp toast cradling griddled steak, crusty rolls enclosing barbecued pork and pita breads stuffed with succulent lamb. But there are also sandwiches of surprising delicacy awaiting discovery, including a contemporized version of the classic B.L.T., an open-faced veal sandwich with caramelized onions and a tart-and-creamy dressing, and a renowned chef's Indian-inspired creation featuring steamed filet mignon.

The following pages, in short, are sure to provide a wealth of meaty inspiration.

Griddled Rib-Eye Steak with Shallot-Wine Sauce & Roquefort Cheese

A traditional French way of finishing off a steak with its own pan juices inspired these robust knife-and-fork sandwiches.

1 tablespoon vegetable oil
1 tablespoon unsalted butter
4 boneless beef rib-eye steaks, 6 to 8 ounces each, trimmed
Salt and freshly ground pepper
4 medium-size shallots, finely chopped
3/4 cup red wine
8 large good-quality sourdough bread slices
1/2 pound soft, creamy Roquefort cheese, at room temperature
2 firm, ripe beefsteak tomatoes, cut into 1/2-inch slices
1 cup packed watercress leaves

In a large, heavy skillet, heat oil and butter over medium to high heat. When butter begins to foam, season steaks generously with salt and pepper and cook in skillet to desired degree of doneness, 3 to 5 minutes per side. When steaks are done, remove from skillet and set aside; pour off all but about 1 tablespoon of fat. Add shallots and sauté until translucent, 1 to 2 minutes. Add wine and, over high heat, stir and scrape with a wooden spoon to dissolve pan deposits; boil briskly until liquid reduces to a glaze, 3 to 5 minutes. Meanwhile, toast bread in a toaster. Spread one side of each slice with cheese. Place 1 slice on each plate and top with steaks. Spoon shallot-wine glaze over meat and top with tomatoes, watercress and remaining bread. Makes 4 servings.

Italian-Style Grilled Flank Steak with Gorgonzola, Arugula, Peperoncini & Tomatoes

Gorgonzola cheese—the mild Italian blue-veined cheese, can be found in specialty cheese shops.

2 tablespoons olive oil
2 tablespoons balsamic vinegar
1 garlic clove, pressed through a garlic press
1-1/2 to 2 pounds beef flank steak, well-trimmed
Salt and freshly ground pepper
8 large slices crusty Italian sourdough bread
Mayonnaise (optional)
Italian-style mustard
6 ounces Gorgonzola cheese, crumbled
4 large peperoncini (Italian pickled peppers), drained and cut diagonally into 1/4-inch-wide strips
4 Roma tomatoes, thinly sliced
3/4 cup packed small arugula leaves

In a shallow bowl large enough to hold steak, stir together oil, vinegar and garlic. Turn steak in mixture and marinate at room temperature 30 minutes, turning several times. Preheat grill or broiler until very hot. Remove steak from marinade, let excess liquid drip off and season meat generously with salt and pepper. Grill to desired degree of doneness, 3 to 5 minutes per side, basting with marinade. Meanwhile, spread one side of each bread slice with mayonnaise, if using, and mustard to taste. Scatter cheese and peperoncini evenly over 4 bread slices. With a carving knife, cut steak into 1/4-inch-thick slices and drape over cheese and peppers. Top with tomato slices, arugula and remaining bread. Makes 4 servings.

Grilled Marinated Flank Steak Sandwich with Chipotle Barbecue Sauce

ERWIN DRECHSLER, METROPOLIS 1800, CHICAGO, ILLINOIS

American bistro fare of the highest order distinguishes the menu at owner/chef Erwin Drechsler's Metropolis 1800. This favorite of the lunchtime menu is served on their own home-baked sesame-olive rolls, but you can substitute your own favorite sandwich roll. Drechsler suggests accompanying it with thick-cut fries and spicy pickles. Canned chipotles, a smoked form of the jalapeño chile, are available in the Latin American or specialty foods sections of well-stocked supermarkets, and in Latin American markets.

1 cup corn oil
3/4 cup mirin (Japanese sweet cooking sake)
1/2 cup soy sauce
3 tablespoons ground star anise
2 tablespoons rice wine vinegar
2 tablespoons grated gingerroot
1 tablespoon ground pepper
2 teaspoons finely chopped garlic
6 (6-oz.) beef flank steaks, trimmed of all fat
Chipotle Barbecue Sauce (see below)
12 red onion slices
6 good-quality sandwich rolls or buns, split
12 Roma tomato slices
6 lettuce leaves

Chipotle Barbecue Sauce
2 canned chipotle chiles, rinsed
1-1/2 red bell peppers, roasted, seeded and peeled (page 2)
1 garlic clove, finely chopped
1/2 cup honey

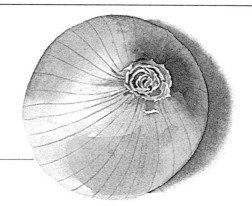

2 tablespoons fresh lime juice
1-1/2 tablespoons grainy Pommery mustard
1 tablespoon peanut oil
1 tablespoon balsamic vinegar
1/2 teaspoon ground cumin
1/2 teaspoon salt
1/2 teaspoon black pepper
1 tablespoon finely chopped fresh cilantro

In a medium-size bowl, stir together oil, mirin, soy sauce, star anise, vinegar, gingerroot, pepper and garlic to make a marinade. One at a time, dunk steaks in marinade and transfer to a shallow rectangular glass dish. Pour marinade over steaks, cover with plastic wrap and refrigerate at least 48 hours or up to 5 days. Prepare Chipotle Barbecue Sauce and refrigerate. Sauce can be refrigerated up to 2 weeks. Preheat grill or broiler until very hot. Remove steaks from marinade, allowing excess liquid to drip off. Grill steaks to desired doneness, 3 to 5 minutes per side; 3 minutes before steaks are done, lightly brush onions with a little oil and grill until golden. Remove steaks and onions and let steaks rest about 2 minutes. Meanwhile, toast split sides of rolls on grill or under broiler. Brush both roll halves generously with barbecue sauce. With a sharp knife, thinly slice steak across the grain and arrange slices on rolls; top with onions, tomato and lettuce. Makes 6 servings.

Chipotle Barbecue Sauce
Put all ingredients except cilantro in a food processor with the metal blade and process until smoothly pureed. Transfer to a bowl and stir in cilantro.

Grilled Sirloin & Sharp Cheddar on Garlic Toast

I imagine this kind of knife-and-fork sandwich being served in an old-fashioned steakhouse—the kind that serves the barest of high-quality basics. If you want to make it more elaborate, prepare a batch of the Sherried Mushrooms on page 109 and spoon them between the meat and cheese. Offer guests your favorite steak sauce, ketchup and mustard on the side. Incidentally, even if you use a grill to cook the steak, you'll still need a preheated broiler to melt the cheese.

1-1/2 to 2 pounds prime beef sirloin steak, trimmed
Salt and freshly ground pepper
Garlic Toast (see below)
1/2 pound sharp Cheddar cheese, thinly sliced
2 tablespoons finely chopped fresh Italian parsley
2 tablespoons finely chopped fresh chives

Garlic Toast
1/4 cup unsalted butter, softened
2 tablespoons finely grated Parmesan cheese
2 garlic cloves, crushed with a garlic press
8 thick slices French or sourdough bread

Preheat grill and/or broiler until very hot. Season steak to taste with salt and pepper and grill close to heat to desired degree of doneness, 6 to 10 minutes for rare to medium-rare, depending on thickness. Remove steak and let rest while completing preparation for Garlic Toast. When toast is ready, cut steak into 1/4- to 1/2-inch-thick slices and arrange on toast. Drape cheese slices over steak and place under broiler just until cheese begins to melt, about 30 seconds. Garnish with parsley and chives and serve immediately. Makes 4 servings.

Garlic Toast

Preheat broiler until very hot. In a small bowl, mash butter, cheese and garlic together with a fork until smoothly blended. Place bread slices on broiler tray and toast until golden on one side. Just before serving, turn bread over, spread untoasted sides evenly with butter mixture and broil until golden-brown.

Steamed Filet Mignon Sandwich with Banana-Mint Salad

John Sedlar, Bikini, Santa Monica, California

My friend John Sedlar, who pioneered Modern Southwest Cuisine at Saint-Estephe restaurant in Manhattan Beach, California, has taken on the world with his new restaurant, Bikini. His interests in the Pacific Rim, and in exploring ever-simpler and fresher ways to prepare and serve food, manifest themselves in this unusual open-faced sandwich made with steamed prime beef. He serves it on pretzel bread—a pretzel-like dough baked in loaf form—made by neighboring chef and baker Hans Rockenwagner; you can substitute any good-quality, dense-textured white bread.

1/2 cup plain lowfat yogurt
4 teaspoons finely chopped fresh mint
2 teaspoons honey
2/3 teaspoon ground cumin
2 ripe bananas, cut into 1/4-inch slices
4 beef filet mignon steaks, about 5 ounces each
4 good-quality white bread slices
4 mint sprigs, for garnish

In a medium-size bowl, stir together yogurt, mint, honey and cumin. Fold in bananas, cover with plastic wrap and refrigerate 1 hour. Preheat broiler or grill. In a steamer or a large pot with a steaming rack, bring 1 inch of water to a full boil. Place filets on steaming rack and steam until medium-rare, 4 to 5 minutes. Meanwhile, grill or broil bread until golden. Place a bread slice on each warmed serving plate. Spoon about two thirds of banana salad on bread. With a sharp knife, cut filets into 1/4- to 1/2-inch-thick slices and drape over salad. Spoon remaining salad attractively over steak and garnish with mint sprigs. Makes 4 servings.

Beefeaters with Horseradish Cream & Tomato

*Plan on serving your leftover roast beef, or good-quality
deli-bought beef, in this combination sauced with the classic
English accompaniment—horseradish cream.*

Horseradish Cream (see below)
8 thin slices pumpernickel or dense brown bread
1 pound thinly sliced cold roast beef
1 beefsteak tomato, or 3 Roma tomatoes, thinly sliced
1/2 cup packed watercress leaves, coarsely chopped

Horseradish Cream
1/2 cup whipping cream, well chilled
1 to 2 tablespoons finely grated fresh horseradish
1 teaspoon cider vinegar
1/2 teaspoon sugar
Salt and white pepper

Prepare Horseradish Cream. Thinly spread one side of each bread slice with Horseradish Cream. Evenly layer roast beef on half the bread slices and lightly spread with a little more sauce. Layer tomato slices on top, then watercress, and top with remaining bread. Cut diagonally in halves. Makes 4 servings.

Horseradish Cream
In a small bowl, use a wire whisk or electric beater to whip cream to stiff peaks. Stir in 1 tablespoon horseradish, vinegar and sugar. Add remaining horseradish to taste, along with salt and pepper. Cover with plastic wrap and refrigerate until using.

Stilton Burgers with Port Wine Mayonnaise

Sweet port wine, a classic after-dinner companion to Stilton, adds a wonderful new dimension to the dressing for these elegant blue-cheese-stuffed burgers. Serve them on good-quality buns of your choice, preferably freshly baked rather than prepackaged.

Port Wine Mayonnaise (see below)
2 pounds lean ground beef
2 medium-size shallots, finely chopped
1/4 cup finely chopped fresh Italian parsley
1/2 pound creamy Stilton cheese, at room temperature
Salt and freshly ground pepper
4 large hamburger buns
4 teaspoons finely chopped fresh chives

Port Wine Mayonnaise
5 tablespoons good-quality mayonnaise
1 tablespoon Port wine

Prepare Port Wine Mayonnaise. Preheat grill or broiler until very hot, leaving cooking rack away from heat. In a medium-size bowl, thoroughly blend beef, shallots and parsley. With your hands, form meat into 8 equal balls and flatten into patties slightly wider than buns. Dot cheese evenly over half the patties to within 1/2 inch of their edges. Top with remaining patties and gently press and crimp edges to seal in cheese. Spray cooking rack with nonstick cooking spray. Season burgers generously on both sides with salt and pepper and cook close to heat to desired doneness, 3 to 5 minutes per side. Generously spread both halves of each bun with Port Wine Mayonnaise, sprinkle with chives and place burgers in buns. Makes 4 servings.

Port Wine Mayonnaise
In a small bowl, stir together mayonnaise and Port until well blended. Cover and refrigerate until used.

Peppercorn Burgers with Brandy Glaze & Parmesan Shavings

Classic pepper steak inspired these flavorful, classy burgers. You'll need a good-quality adjustable pepper mill to grind the pepper just right. Buy the best Parmesan cheese you can find, in block form, and shave it yourself using a cheese slicer or the slicing slot on a hand-held grater.

2 pounds lean ground beef
Salt
Whole peppercorns
1 tablespoon vegetable oil
1 tablespoon unsalted butter
1/4 pound Parmesan cheese, cut into very thin shavings
1/4 cup brandy
4 large hamburger buns
Creamy Dijon-style mustard
4 beefsteak tomato slices

With your hands, form meat into 4 equal patties slightly larger than diameters of buns. Season with salt on both sides. Put peppercorns in a pepper grinder and adjust grinder to coarsest setting—usually achieved by loosening bolt at top of grinder. Grind pepper generously over both sides of burgers and gently pat into surfaces. In a large skillet, heat oil and butter over medium to high heat. When butter foams, add burgers and cook to desired degree of doneness, 3 to 5 minutes per side; after turning burgers, top with Parmesan shavings. Remove burgers from skillet and set aside; pour off all but about 1 tablespoon of fat from skillet. Away from heat, add brandy and stir and scrape with a wooden spoon to dissolve pan deposits. Return to heat and simmer briskly until brandy reduces to a glaze, 1 to 2 minutes. Spread both halves of each bun with mustard to taste, place burgers on buns, spoon glaze over burgers and top with tomato. Makes 4 servings.

Deli-Style Roast Beef with Swiss Cheese, Slaw & Thousand Island Dressing

You'll find all the fixings for this in any good-quality delicatessen.
Make them larger or smaller, depending on your appetite and how wide
you can open your mouth! Serve with dill pickle spears.

8 rye bread slices
Deli-style mustard of choice (optional)
1 to 1-1/2 pounds lean roast beef, thinly sliced
1/2 to 3/4 cup thousand island dressing
1 to 1-1/2 cups deli-style cole slaw, drained of excess liquid
6 ounces Swiss cheese, thinly sliced
4 small Roma tomatoes, thinly sliced

Spread one side of each bread slice with mustard to taste, if using. Arrange beef in neat, even layers on 4 slices. Spread about half of dressing evenly over beef, to taste. Arrange cole slaw on top, then a layer of cheese, tomatoes, more dressing and remaining bread. Gently press down on sandwiches and cut in halves. Makes 4 servings.

Classic Deli Club

I love the classic delicatessen combination of corned beef and chopped liver—the way the lean meatiness and salty taste of the beef combines with the smooth richness of the pureed liver. All the basic ingredients are available at the take-out counter of any good deli. Serve with sour dill pickles.

12 rye bread slices
Deli-style mustard
1-1/2 pounds thinly sliced lean corned beef or pastrami
1/2 cup Russian or thousand island dressing
3/4 pint deli-made chopped liver
1 cup deli-made cole slaw, drained of excess dressing
6 ounces thinly sliced Swiss cheese

Spread one side of each bread slice to taste with mustard. Arrange corned beef in even layers on 4 slices. Spoon dressing generously over meat. Spread liver evenly on mustard side of 4 more slices and place, liver-side up, on top of meat and dressing. Arrange cole slaw evenly on top of liver and top with cheese and remaining bread. Cut into halves and serve. Makes 4 servings.

Reuben Melt

Buy the best-quality delicatessen ingredients you can find for this griddled version of a lunchtime classic. Several layers of shredded cheese help hold the sandwich together. Serve with dill pickle spears and French fries or potato chips.

6 tablespoons unsalted butter, softened
8 rye bread slices
Sweet-hot deli-style mustard or other good-quality mustard
1/2 pound Swiss, Gruyere or Emmenthaler cheese, coarsely shredded
1 pound thinly sliced lean pastrami
1 cup sauerkraut, very well drained

Spread butter evenly on one side of each bread slice. Turn slices buttered sides down and spread to taste with mustard. Sprinkle about a quarter of the cheese in even layers on top of mustard on 4 bread slices. Evenly layer half of pastrami on top. Sprinkle another quarter of cheese over pastrami and top with an even layer of sauerkraut. Add another quarter of cheese, remaining pastrami and remaining cheese, finishing with remaining bread slices placed buttered sides up. Spray a large, heavy skillet with nonstick cooking spray and heat over medium heat. Add sandwiches and fry, pressing down frequently and firmly with the back of a spatula, until undersides are golden-brown, 3 to 4 minutes. Carefully turn sandwiches over and fry, pressing frequently, 3 to 4 minutes more. Cut into halves and serve. Makes 4 servings.

Italian Sandwich

BRIAN GALLAGHER, KYLA'S, ROYAL OAK, MICHIGAN

Housed in a former art gallery, the restaurant chef Brian Gallagher runs with his wife Simona makes good food an approachable artform in its own right—witness Brian's casual-yet-elegant take on a traditional Italian theme. He suggests serving it with a chilled pasta salad containing a mixture of pesto, sun-dried tomatoes, feta cheese, ripe pepper and a touch of olive oil. Most well-stocked supermarkets and Italian delis sell containers of ready-to-use pesto sauce.

4 large slices Italian bread
1/4 cup olive oil
1/2 cup pesto
1-1/4 pounds hard Italian salami, thinly sliced and cut into julienne strips
1 pound fresh spinach leaves, stemmed, thoroughly washed and cut into julienne
   strips
1/2 pound red onion, thinly sliced
3/4 pound Gruyere cheese, thinly sliced
24 sun-dried tomato pieces
1/4 pound feta cheese, crumbled

Preheat oven to 350°F (175°C). Place bread slices on individual ovenproof metal or ceramic dishes and drizzle with olive oil. Spread pesto on each slice. In a medium-size bowl, toss together salami, spinach and onion. Arrange mixture on top of bread and top with Gruyere cheese slices. Place sun-dried tomatoes on top of Gruyere cheese and sprinkle with feta cheese. Bake in preheated oven until sandwiches are heated through and cheese is melted and bubbling, 10 to 15 minutes. Makes 4 servings.

Veal Tenderloin with Lemon-Dijon Cream & Caramelized Onions

Slowly sautéed until golden, the onions in these open-faced sandwiches highlight the sweet, mild flavor of good-quality veal.

Caramelized Onions (see below)
Lemon-Dijon Cream (see below)
4 boneless saddles of veal, about 6 ounces each
Salt and white pepper
4 good-quality multi-grain or whole-wheat bread slices
1 tablespoon finely chopped fresh chives
1 tablespoon finely chopped fresh Italian parsley

Caramelized Onions

2 tablespoons unsalted butter
2 tablespoons olive oil
2 medium-size sweet Maui, Vidalia, Walla Walla or red onions, cut into 1/4-inch-thick slices
2 teaspoons cider vinegar

Lemon-Dijon Cream

2 tablespoons lemon juice
1 teaspoon grainy Dijon-style mustard
1/2 cup whipping cream
Salt and white pepper

Prepare Caramelized Onion and Lemon-Dijon Cream. Preheat broiler or grill until very hot. Season veal with salt and pepper and grill or broil close to heat until medium done, still slightly pink in middle, 3 to 4 minutes per side. Remove from heat and set aside. Meanwhile, toast bread on grill or under broiler until golden. Spread onions on one side of each slice and place each slice on an individual serving plate. With a carving knife, cut

veal diagonally into 1/4-inch-thick slices and arrange on top of onions. Drizzle veal with Lemon-Dijon Cream and garnish with chives and parsley. Makes 4 servings.

Caramelized Onions

In a medium-size saucepan, heat butter and oil over low to medium heat. Add onions and sauté, stirring frequently, until uniformly golden-brown, 15 to 20 minutes. Add vinegar and, with a wooden spoon, stir and scrape to dissolve any pan deposits.

Lemon-Dijon Cream

In a small bowl, stir together lemon juice and mustard with a wire whisk or fork. Stirring briskly, slowly pour in cream to form a thick sauce. Add salt and pepper to taste.

Charred Lamb Sandwich with Curry Aïoli

MICHAEL FOLEY, PRINTER'S ROW, CHICAGO, ILLINOIS

At Printer's Row, Chicago restaurateur Michael Foley inventively combines good local ingredients with styles of cooking from around the world to forge a uniquely Midwestern version of new American cuisine. His flavorful sandwich of Cajun-seasoned leg of lamb is sauced with an aïoli—the traditional Provençal garlic mayonnaise— that is alluringly flavored with East Indian spices. He suggests accompanying the sandwiches with a salad of sliced cucumbers dressed with yogurt.

Curry Aïoli (see below)
1 pound boneless leg of lamb, trimmed of fat and sinew, at room temperature
Salt
1 large garlic clove, cut in half
3 tablespoons olive oil
1 tablespoon commercial Cajun-style seasoning mix (MSG-free)
1 teaspoon finely chopped fresh rosemary
1 teaspoon finely chopped fresh thyme
8 eggplant slices, about 1/4 inch thick
8 whole-wheat or multi-grain bread slices
8 beefsteak tomato slices, about 1/4 inch thick

Curry Aïoli

3 egg yolks, at room temperature
2 garlic cloves, minced
1-1/2 tablespoons seedless raisins, plumped in warm water 10 minutes, then drained
1 cup extra-virgin olive oil
1 tablespoon curry powder
2 teaspoons fine bread crumbs
1/2 teaspoon salt
1-1/2 tablespoons chicken broth

Prepare Curry Aïoli. Preheat oven to 350°F (175°C). Season lamb lightly and evenly with salt, rub all over with cut sides of garlic and then rub on 2 tablespoons oil. In a small bowl, stir together Cajun seasoning, rosemary and thyme, then spread mixture on work surface and roll lamb in seasonings until well coated. Over high heat, heat a cast-iron skillet large enough to hold lamb comfortably. Add lamb to dry skillet and cook until surface is uniformly charred, 3 to 4 minutes total. Transfer lamb in skillet to preheated oven and cook until medium-rare to medium, 12 to 15 minutes. Remove lamb from skillet and let rest at room temperature 5 to 10 minutes. Brush eggplant slices with remaining oil. In a lightweight skillet over medium heat, sauté eggplant until translucent and lightly golden, 2 to 3 minutes per side. Spread one side of each bread slice with aioli to taste. Layer tomato and eggplant on half the slices. With a carving knife, cut lamb into thin slices and arrange on top. Add remaining bread and, if desired, cut sandwiches into halves. Makes 4 servings.

Curry Aïoli

In a food processor with the metal blade, process egg yolks, garlic and raisins until smooth. With machine running, slowly pour olive oil through the feed tube in a thin, steady stream; sauce will mound and thicken like mayonnaise. Add curry powder, bread crumbs and salt; process to combine. Thin to spreading consistency with the broth.

Greek Lamb Sandwiches with Basil-Garlic Spread, Ripe Olives & Feta

*Though the quality of the ingredients called for have a certain elegance
to them, the flavor combination is traditionally rustic Greek—and demands
being eaten in a plain or whole-wheat pita bread. The spread pares pesto
down to its barest essentials—basil, garlic and olive oil.*

6 tablespoons olive oil
1/3 cup packed fresh basil leaves
1 garlic clove, peeled
4 (6-oz.) lamb tenderloins
Salt and freshly ground pepper
4 plain or whole-wheat pita breads
3/4 cup Greek-style marinated ripe olives, pitted
1/2 pound feta cheese, coarsely crumbled
1-1/2 cups coarsely shredded butter lettuce
4 small Roma tomatoes, thinly sliced

Preheat grill or broiler until very hot. In a food processor with the metal blade, put 1/4 cup olive oil, basil and garlic. Process until smoothly pureed. Set aside. Rub lamb with remaining oil and season generously with salt and pepper. Grill to desired degree of doneness, 3 to 5 minutes per side. Set lamb aside and warm pitas on grill or under broiler, 1/2 to 1 minute per side. With a small, sharp knife, slit one long side of each pita to open it like a pocket. Generously spread basil sauce inside pockets. Slice lamb crosswise into thin slices and toss with olives and feta. Arrange bed of lettuce and tomato inside each pita and stuff with lamb mixture. Makes 4 servings.

Roasted Lambwiches with Mint-Jelly Mayonnaise

If you're fond of lamb's traditional mint-jelly accompaniment, this is a terrific, easy way to use up leftover roast or grilled meat. It's even worth buying and cooking a little extra so you'll have enough for sandwiches the next day.

8 crusty white or whole-wheat bread slices
1/4 cup mayonnaise
2 tablespoons mint jelly
1 pound cold leftover roast or grilled lamb, trimmed and thinly sliced
2 large Roma tomatoes, thinly sliced
4 large radicchio or red-leaf lettuce leaves

Toast the bread until golden-brown. In a small bowl, stir together mayonnaise and mint jelly. Spread generously on one side of each bread slice. Arrange sliced lamb on 4 slices of bread, then top with tomato slices, radicchio or lettuce and remaining bread. Cut into halves before serving. Makes 4 servings.

Chinese Honey-Grilled Pork with Hoisin Mustard & Fried Green Onions

Vividly Asian flavors pay court to the naturally sweet and meaty flavor of pork in this easy-to-make yet elegant sandwich. If you're cutting down on fried foods, substitute fresh, raw slivers of green onions. Sweet pickled crabapples make a wonderful garnish.

1/4 cup honey
1/4 cup Chinese soy sauce
1/2 tablespoon grated gingerroot
1/2 teaspoon ground star anise
2 pounds pork tenderloin
Salt and pepper
3 tablespoons Chinese hoisin sauce
1 teaspoon prepared hot mustard
Fried Green Onions (see below)
4 soft, fresh-baked sandwich rolls, split
2 large Roma tomatoes, thinly sliced

Fried Green Onions
2 medium-size green onions
Vegetable oil for deep-frying

In a shallow glass or ceramic dish, stir together honey, soy sauce, gingerroot and star anise. Turn pork tenderloin in mixture, cover with plastic wrap and refrigerate 1 to 2 hours. Preheat grill or broiler until very hot. Remove pork from marinade, season well with salt and pepper and grill close to heat, basting frequently with marinade, until done, about 7 minutes for medium. In a small bowl, stir together hoisin sauce and mustard and spread on both sides of rolls. Prepare Fried Green Onions. Thinly slice pork on the

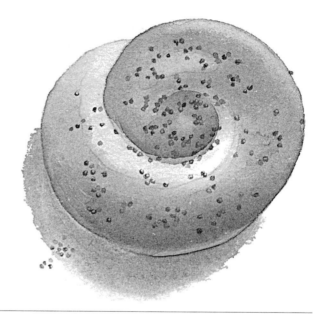

diagonal and arrange slices on bottoms of rolls. Place tomato slices on pork, then top with green onions and top halves of rolls. Makes 4 servings.

Fried Green Onions

With a small, sharp knife, trim green onions and cut lengthwise into thin slivers about 1/8 inch wide and 1 to 2 inches long. In a heavy skillet, heat about 1 inch of oil to 250°F (120°C) on a deep-frying thermometer. Scatter green onions into hot oil and fry, sub-merging frequently with a wire skimmer, until golden-brown, about 10 minutes. Remove with skimmer and spread on several layers of paper towels to drain.

Molasses Barbecued Pork

MICHAEL MCCARTY, MICHAEL'S, LOS ANGELES AND NEW YORK CITY

I had the great good fortune to work as writer on Michael's Cookbook (Macmillan, 1989), from the amazingly energetic and creative cook and entrepreneur Michael McCarty. While he's known as one of the pioneers of California cuisine, this sandwich—adapted from the recipe that appears in his book—is an old-fashioned favorite he serves at brunch, based on a recipe Michael's parents used to make. He recommends a good commercial tomato-and-molasses barbecue sauce. Michael serves the sandwiches with a salad of mixed baby greens dressed with a balsamic vinaigrette.

2-1/2 pounds pork tenderloin
4 cups tomato-molasses-based commercial barbecue sauce
3/4 cup molasses
1/4 cup strong black coffee
Juice of 1 lime
1 small Maui, Walla Walla, Vidalia or sweet red onion, finely chopped
2 medium-size garlic cloves, finely chopped
1 small red bell pepper, finely chopped
1 small yellow bell pepper, finely chopped
1 medium-size jalapeño chile, roasted, peeled, seeded and finely chopped (page 2)
Salt and freshly ground white pepper
1 medium-size Maui onion, cut into 1/4-inch-thick slices
3/4 cup melted butter
6 tablespoons Jalapeño-Cilantro-Lime Salsa (see below)
2 sourdough baguettes, each 18 inches long, or 6 sourdough rolls, each 6 inches long
2 bunches watercress leaves, coarsely chopped

Jalapeño-Cilantro-Lime Salsa
1/2 cup extra-virgin olive oil
1 jalapeño chile, roasted, peeled, seeded and finely chopped (page 2)
1 tablespoon finely chopped fresh cilantro leaves
Salt and freshly ground white pepper
1 lime, cut in half

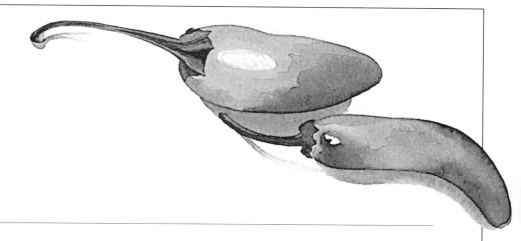

Start marinating pork as early as the night before, but no later than 45 minutes before cooking. In a bowl, stir together 3 cups barbecue sauce, molasses, coffee, lime juice, chopped onion, garlic, bell peppers and jalapeño. Put pork in bowl, turning to coat it well; cover with plastic wrap and leave in refrigerator to marinate at least 45 minutes or as long as overnight. Before cooking, preheat grill or broiler until very hot. Wipe marinade from pork, saving marinade, and lightly season meat with salt and pepper. Grill pork 5 to 7 minutes per side or until no longer pink in center, basting frequently with marinade. About 3 minutes before pork is done, lightly brush onion slices with some butter, sprinkle with salt and pepper, and grill about 1-1/2 minutes per side. Prepare Jalapeño-Cilantro-Lime Salsa. Cut each sourdough baguette into 3 (6-inch) pieces and halve bread lengthwise. Brush cut sides with butter and toast on grill as pork finishes cooking. Lightly brush bottom halves of toasted bread with some of remaining barbecue sauce and arrange watercress leaves on top. Cut pork diagonally into 1/4-inch-thick slices and place on top of watercress; spoon salsa over pork. Arrange grilled onions on top of pork and spoon more sauce over onions and pork. Top with other halves bread tops and cut each sandwich in half before serving. Makes 6 servings.

Jalapeño-Cilantro-Lime Salsa

In a bowl, stir together olive oil, jalapeño and cilantro. Season to taste with salt and pepper. Just before using, squeeze in lime and stir well. (Lime juice will discolor cilantro if added earlier.) Makes about 1/2 cup.

Indonesian Satay-Style Pork with Sweet-Sour Vegetables & Spicy Peanut Sauce

The Indonesian appetizer skewers known as satay inspired these satisfying open-faced sandwiches, topped with a satisfying warm and spicy peanut sauce.

2 tablespoons soy sauce
1 tablespoon lime juice
1 tablespoon lemon juice
1 tablespoon honey
1 tablespoon peanut oil
1 tablespoon sesame oil
1/2 teaspoon Chinese five-spice powder
1 small hot green chile, finely chopped
1 garlic clove, crushed
1 shallot, finely chopped
1-1/2 pounds pork tenderloin, trimmed
Sweet-Sour Vegetables (see below)
Spicy Peanut Sauce (see following page)
4 large, thick slices pumpernickel bread
2 tablespoons finely chopped fresh cilantro

Sweet-Sour Vegetables
1/4 cup Japanese rice vinegar
1 teaspoon sugar
1 teaspoon salt
1 medium-size Japanese cucumber, very thinly sliced
1 medium-size red onion, very thinly sliced
1 medium-size carrot, thinly shredded

Spicy Peanut Sauce
1 medium-size garlic clove, pressed through a garlic press
1 small hot red or green chile, seeded and very finely chopped
1 teaspoon finely grated gingerroot
1/2 teaspoon Thai fish sauce (nam pla)
1 tablespoon peanut oil
1 cup crunchy-style peanut butter
1/2 cup cold water
1-1/2 tablespoons canned coconut cream
1 tablespoon lime or lemon juice

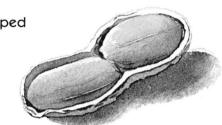

In a medium-size bowl, stir together soy sauce, lime and lemon juices, honey, peanut and sesame oils, five-spice powder, chile, garlic and shallot. Add pork, cover with plastic wrap and marinate in refrigerator 2 hours. As soon as pork starts marinating, prepare Sweet-Sour Vegetables. Remove pork from refrigerator 1/2 hour before cooking and let come to room temperature. Preheat grill or broiler until very hot. Prepare Spicy Peanut Sauce and keep warm. Remove pork from marinade and grill until no longer pink in center, 5 to 7 minutes per side. Place a slice of bread on each serving plate. Drain vegetables well and arrange in even beds on top of bread. With a sharp knife, cut pork into 1/4-inch-thick slices. Drape pork over vegetables. Drizzle peanut sauce over pork and garnish with cilantro. Makes 4 servings.

Sweet-Sour Vegetables
In a glass or ceramic bowl, stir together vinegar, sugar and salt. Add vegetables, toss well, cover with plastic wrap and refrigerate until serving.

Spicy Peanut Sauce
In a small bowl, stir together garlic, chile, gingerroot and fish sauce. In a saucepan, heat oil over medium heat. Add contents of bowl and cook, stirring, 1 minute. Reduce heat slightly and add remaining ingredients. Cook, stirring continuously, until smooth and heated through.

Ultimate Italian Sausage Grinder

I've always found Italian sausage sandwiches kind of awkward to eat:
One bite, and you pull a whole sausage, or at least a large chunk, out of the roll.
This version solves the problem by skinning the sausage and sautéing it in rough
chunks, which are tossed with a colorful array of roasted peppers—and a splash
of good balsamic vinegar to cut the greasiness—before being stuffed into individual
rolls. The filling may also be stuffed into pita breads.

4 large individual Italian rolls
1/2 cup mayonnaise
1 tablespoon olive oil
1-1/2 pounds fresh sweet or hot Italian sausage, or a mixture, casings removed
3 red, yellow or green bell peppers, roasted, peeled (page 2) and torn into strips,
   juices reserved
2 tablespoons balsamic vinegar
1-1/2 tablespoons finely chopped Italian parsley
12 to 16 small butter lettuce leaves

With a bread knife, split rolls lengthwise, taking care not to cut all the way through. Open rolls and, with your fingers, pull out bread to a 1/2-inch depth all along both sides. Spread generously with mayonnaise and set aside. Heat oil in a large, heavy skillet over medium to high heat. Add sausage, breaking it into large bite-size chunks, and sauté until evenly, lightly browned, 2 to 3 minutes. Carefully pour off all but about 1 table-spoon of fat from skillet. Return to heat and add bell peppers with their juices and bal-samic vinegar. Stir and scrape with wooden spoon to dissolve pan deposits. Continue simmering briskly until liquid reduces to a glaze, 2 to 3 minutes more. Toss in parsley and spoon mixture into rolls. Top with lettuce leaves and serve whole or cut into halves. Makes 4 servings.

Nouvelle B.L.T.

Contemporary variations on the classic ingredients bestow distinction on this refined version of a diner favorite. While you can use standard streaky supermarket bacon, it's worth seeking out a good-quality smoked bacon such as the variety called for below.

Sun-Dried Tomato Mayonnaise (see below)
8 good-quality, dense white or sourdough bread slices
16 applewood-smoked bacon slices, crisp-cooked
8 arugula leaves
8 small or 4 large butter lettuce leaves

Sun-Dried Tomato Mayonnaise
8 pieces oil-packed sun-dried tomatoes, drained
5 tablespoons mayonnaise
2 teaspoons lemon juice

Prepare Sun-Dried Tomato Mayonnaise. In a toaster or under the broiler, toast bread until golden. Generously spread one side of each slice with Sun-Dried Tomato Mayonnaise. Arrange bacon across 4 slices and top with arugula and lettuce, then remaining bread. Cut sandwiches diagonally into halves. Makes 4 servings.

Sun-Dried Tomato Mayonnaise
Put all ingredients in a food processor with the metal blade and process until smooth. Cover with plastic wrap and refrigerate until ready to use.

Pork Burgers with Cider-Mustard Mayonnaise & Gruyere

A tangy mayonnaise flavored with cider vinegar and mustard, along with a topping of nutty-flavored cheese, complements the naturally sweet flavor of ground pork.

Cider-Mustard Mayonnaise (see below)
2 pounds lean ground pork
1/2 teaspoon ground allspice
Salt and freshly ground black pepper
6 ounces Gruyere or Emmenthaler cheese, thinly sliced
4 large hamburger buns
3/4 cup packed watercress leaves

Cider-Mustard Mayonnaise
1/4 cup mayonnaise
1 tablespoon creamy Dijon-style mustard
2 teaspoons cider vinegar

Prepare Cider-Mustard Mayonnaise. Preheat barbecue, grill or broiler until very hot, leaving cooking rack away from heat. In a medium-size bowl, thoroughly blend pork and allspice. With your hands, form meat into 4 patties slightly wider than buns. Spray cooking rack with nonstick cooking spray. Season burgers generously on both sides with salt and pepper and cook close to heat until no longer pink in center, 4 to 5 minutes per side; if using a grill, top burgers with cheese just after turning; if broiling, add cheese about 30 seconds before burgers are done. Toast split sides of buns on grill or under broiler and generously spread both halves with Cider-Mustard Mayonnaise. Place burgers in buns and top with watercress. Makes 4 servings.

Cider-Mustard Mayonnaise
In a small bowl, stir together all ingredients. Cover with plastic wrap and refrigerate until ready to use.

Ham & Gruyere Cheese with Sweet Pickles & Hot Mustard

To me, the ideal take on ham-and-cheese pairs a good-quality, sweetly cured and cooked ham with an equally sweet and mellow-flavored Gruyere cheese. Sweet pickled cucumbers and the hottest mustard you can stand provide the perfect finishing touches. If you like, you can also spread the outer sides of the bread with butter, distribute the cheese evenly on both sides of the ham and grill the sandwiches, as described in the recipe for Reuben Melt on page 18.

8 rye or sourdough bread slices
Hot deli-style mustard
1 pound thinly sliced smoked, cooked ham
2 large sweet pickled cucumbers, cut crosswise into thin slices
6 ounces thinly sliced Gruyere cheese

Spread one side of each bread slice to taste with mustard. Evenly layer ham on half the bread slices. Top with an even layer of pickle slices, then cheese and remaining bread. Cut into halves. Makes 4 servings.

Prosciutto & Smoked Provolone

The intense salty-sweet flavor of Italian prosciutto—the raw, dry-cured ham from Parma, available in any good Italian or gourmet deli—finds a great companion in smoked provolone cheese. Make sure to ask that both be cut tissue-thin for you. They're used somewhat sparingly in these sandwiches—the better for their flavors and textures to be appreciated. Serve with peperoncini—pale yellow-green Italian pickled peppers.

8 dense brown bread, rye or pumpernickel-raisin slices
Good-quality deli-style mustard
Mayonnaise
1/2 pound prosciutto, cut into tissue-thin slices
Freshly ground black pepper
1/4 pound very thinly sliced smoked provolone cheese

Thinly spread one side of each bread slice with mustard and mayonnaise. Drape prosciutto on half the bread slices and grind black pepper to taste over meat. Top with cheese and remaining bread. Cut diagonally into halves. Makes 4 servings.

Muffelata with Creole Mayonnaise

The Creole kitchen's answer to the submarine or hero sandwich, this generous creation may be varied to suit your taste, adding your favorite meats and garnishes. It makes a great centerpiece for casual entertaining: Make several in advance and place them on a carving board with a bread knife, for guests to slice and serve themselves.

Creole Mayonnaise (see below)
1 large loaf crusty French bread, about 2 feet long
1 pound thinly sliced cured ham
4 large Roma tomatoes, thinly sliced
1 pound thinly sliced spicy salami
1 large red onion, very thinly sliced
1 pound thinly sliced roast beef
1-1/2 cups shredded butter lettuce

Creole Mayonnaise
1/2 cup mayonnaise
2 tablespoons finely chopped fresh chives
2 teaspoons grated lemon zest
1/4 teaspoon red (cayenne) pepper
4 to 6 drops hot pepper sauce

Prepare Creole Mayonnaise. With a bread knife, cut lengthwise along French bread, splitting it open without slicing all the way through. With your fingers, pull out about a 1-inch depth of bread all along both sides of loaf. Generously spread inside of bread on both sides with mayonnaise. Evenly layer ham on bottom half and top with tomatoes. Then layer salami and top with onion. Finally, layer beef and top with lettuce. Close top over filling to completely enclose it, pressing loaf securely shut. To serve, cut into sections. Makes 4 servings.

Creole Mayonnaise
In a small bowl, stir together all ingredients. Cover with plastic wrap and refrigerate until ready to use.

Uptown Meatloaf Burgers with Spicy Ketchup

My grandmother couldn't make a hamburger without adding herbs and spices to it. At the time, I preferred them plain. But with the renewed interest in old-fashioned comfort foods that saw fancy restaurants adding meatloaf to their menus, I began to see the virtues in making well-seasoned, succulent meat patties. Feel free to vary the proportion of the meats to your taste and to alter the shape of the burgers to fit a bread different from the rolls suggested. And make a few extra of these, if you like, to serve cold the next day—in traditional meatloaf fashion.

Spicy Tomato Ketchup (see below)
1 pound lean ground beef
1/2 pound ground veal
1/2 pound lean ground pork
1 egg
1 green or red bell pepper, roasted, peeled (page 2) and finely diced
1 small red onion, finely chopped
1/4 cup soft white bread crumbs
2 tablespoons tomato ketchup
1 tablespoon finely chopped fresh Italian parsley
1/2 tablespoon dried leaf oregano
Salt and freshly ground black pepper
4 large onion or kaiser rolls, split
Mayonnaise (optional)
4 large beefsteak tomato slices
4 butter or red-leaf lettuce leaves

Spicy Tomato Ketchup
6 tablespoons bottled tomato ketchup
1 to 2 teaspoons finely grated fresh or bottled horseradish
1/4 to 1/2 teaspoon dry mustard powder
3 to 6 drops hot pepper sauce

Prepare Spicy Tomato Ketchup. Preheat grill or broiler until very hot. In a medium-size bowl, use your fingers to mix together beef, veal, pork, egg, bell pepper, onion, bread crumbs, ketchup, parsley and oregano. With your hands, form meat mixture into 4 patties slightly wider than buns. Season burgers generously on both sides with salt and black pepper and cook close to heat until medium done, 4 to 5 minutes per side. Toast split sides of buns on grill or under broiler and generously spread both halves with mayonnaise, if using, and Spicy Tomato Ketchup. Place burgers in buns and top with tomato and lettuce. Makes 4 servings.

Spicy Tomato Ketchup

Put ketchup in a small bowl and stir in other ingredients to taste.

Poultry Sandwiches

Time was, a poultry sandwich meant chicken salad or turkey on rye. But today's health-conscious eaters demand a wider range of poultry choices—a trend that gives rise to the diverse recipes that follow.

Not surprisingly, chicken breasts—flavorful, adaptable and conveniently portioned—figure prominently. The selections don't stop there, though. Check out the spicy dark-meat grilled chicken sandwich created by an innovative Arizona chef. And don't miss the chicken burgers that cast a favorite double-decker in a fresh new light.

Of course, you'll also find turkey sandwiches galore, featuring freshly cooked, deli-sliced and leftover meats.

Grilled Chicken with Sun-Dried Tomato Pesto, Eggplant & Goat Cheese

A trio of Italian-inspired favorites adds zest to marinated chicken breast in this bright and flavorful sandwich. Pumpernickel or black bread provides a good, earthy background for the lively flavors; sourdough would also be good.

Sun-Dried Tomato Pesto (see below)
1/4 cup olive oil
1/4 cup lemon juice
1 tablespoon dried leaf oregano
4 large boneless, skinless chicken breast halves
Salt and pepper
1/2 pound eggplant, peeled and cut into 1/4-inch-thick slices
8 pumpernickel or brown bread slices
1/2 pound fresh creamy goat cheese

Sun-Dried Tomato Pesto

1/4 cup oil-packed sun-dried tomatoes, drained
2 to 3 tablespoons olive oil from tomatoes
1 tablespoon grated Parmesan cheese
1 small garlic clove, peeled

Prepare pesto. In a shallow bowl, stir together oil, lemon juice and oregano. Turn chicken breasts in mixture and marinate at room temperature about 30 minutes. Preheat grill or broiler until very hot. Remove chicken from marinade, reserving marinade. Season chicken with salt and pepper and grill or broil close to heat until no longer pink in center, 4 to 5 minutes per side. During last 2 to 3 minutes of cooking, dip eggplant slices in marinade and grill or broil until golden, 1 to 1-1/2 minutes per side. Meanwhile, spread one side of 4 bread slices with goat cheese; spread other slices with pesto. Place chicken

breasts on top of goat cheese, drape with eggplant slices and top with remaining bread. Cut sandwiches into halves. Makes 4 servings.

Sun-Dried Tomato Pesto

In a blender or a food processor with the metal blade, process tomatoes, 2 tablespoons oil, Parmesan and garlic until pureed. Add a little more oil, if necessary, to bring puree to a thick spreading consistency.

Grilled Chicken with Fennel on Focaccia

MICHAEL SHORTINO, TOP OF THE ROCK, THE BUTTES, TEMPE, ARIZONA

It takes a vivid-tasting sandwich to vie with the picture-window views at this Southwestern resort restaurant. While chef Michael Shortino uses his own rosemary focaccia rolls, you can substitute any good quality herb-scented or plain rolls, or squares of traditional Italian-style rosemary-scented focaccia—a fairly flat bread usually sold in rectangular sheets.

1/4 cup plus 1 tablespoon olive oil
2 tablespoons lemon juice
2 garlic cloves, finely chopped
1 teaspoon dried leaf basil
1 teaspoon dried leaf oregano
1 teaspoon dried leaf thyme
1/2 teaspoon salt
4 boneless, skinless chicken breasts, about 1/4 pound each
2 small red onions, thinly sliced
1 fennel bulb, cut into julienne strips
2 Roma tomatoes, cored and thinly sliced
4 sharp provolone cheese slices, 1 to 1-1/2 ounces each
4 focaccia rolls, split
Red wine vinegar
Freshly ground pepper

A full day before serving, stir together 1/4 cup olive oil, lemon juice, 1 garlic clove, basil, oregano, thyme and salt in a shallow dish large enough to hold chicken breasts side by side. Turn chicken in mixture, cover with plastic wrap and marinate in refrigerator 24 hours, turning breasts occasionally. Before serving, preheat grill or broiler until very hot; preheat oven to 350°F (175°C). Grill chicken breasts, 4 to 5 minutes per side. Meanwhile, heat remaining oil in a skillet over medium to high heat and sauté onions, fennel and

remaining garlic until soft and translucent, 4 to 5 minutes. When chicken is almost done, place tomato slices on top and top with cheese. Put rolls in oven to warm 1 to 2 minutes. Place a chicken breast in each roll, top with sautéed vegetables and season to taste with olive oil, red wine vinegar and pepper. Makes 4 servings.

Tandoori Chicken Sandwich with Raita
in Whole-Wheat Pita

With its marinade of spiced low-fat yogurt and its yogurt-and-vegetable dressing, this sandwich is not only flavorful but also remarkably healthy. Whole-wheat pita breads make the ideal containers.

Raita (see below)
1/2 cup plain lowfat yogurt
2 tablespoons fresh lemon juice
1 tablespoon finely grated gingerroot
1 teaspoon ground cardamom
1 teaspoon red (cayenne) pepper
1 teaspoon ground coriander
4 large boneless, skinless chicken breast halves
Salt and white pepper
4 individual-size whole-wheat pita breads
4 large red-leaf or butter lettuce leaves

Raita

1/2 cup plain lowfat yogurt
1 tablespoon lemon juice
1-1/2 tablespoons finely chopped fresh cilantro
1/2 tablespoon finely chopped fresh mint
1/2 teaspoon sugar
2 firm, ripe Roma tomatoes, cored, seeded and coarsely chopped
1 large pickling cucumber, unpeeled, coarsely shredded
1/2 medium-size red onion, finely chopped

Prepare Raita. In a shallow bowl, stir together yogurt, lemon juice and spices. Turn chicken breasts in mixture and marinate at room temperature about 30 minutes. Preheat

grill or broiler until very hot. Remove chicken from yogurt marinade. Season with salt and pepper and grill or broil close to heat until no longer pink in center, 4 to 5 minutes per side. Remove chicken, set aside and grill or broil pita breads until lightly golden but still soft, about 30 seconds per side. With a small, sharp knife, slit breads along one long side. Insert lettuce leaves and place chicken breasts on top of lettuce. Spoon Raita over chicken. Makes 4 servings.

Raita

In a medium-size bowl, stir together yogurt, lemon juice, cilantro, mint and sugar. Fold in vegetables. Cover with plastic wrap and refrigerate.

Taos-Style Grilled Chicken with Green Chiles

Mild green Anaheim chiles—the slender, 6-to-8-inch-long kind often sold in super-market produce sections labeled "green chile" or "chile verde"—add subtle spice and fresh taste to complement the mild red chile powder that flavors grilled chicken. If you can't find fresh chiles, buy the already-roasted canned mild green chiles.

2 tablespoons olive oil
2 tablespoons lime juice
2 tablespoons pure mild chile powder
1 tablespoon dried leaf oregano
4 large boneless, skinless chicken breast halves
Salt and pepper
4 good-quality soft sandwich rolls
4 medium-size mild green Anaheim chiles, roasted, stemmed, seeded and peeled
   (page 2)
1/2 pound Monterey Jack cheese, sliced
1/2 cup mayonnaise
2 tablespoons finely chopped fresh cilantro
4 beefsteak tomato slices
4 red-leaf or butter lettuce leaves

In a small bowl, stir together oil, lime juice, chile powder and oregano to make a fluid paste. Put chicken breasts in a shallow glass or ceramic dish and coat well with paste; cover with plastic wrap, refrigerate and marinate at least 1 or up to 4 hours. Preheat grill or broiler until very hot. Without removing marinade paste, season chicken with salt and pepper and grill or broil close to heat until no longer pink in center, 4 to 5 minutes per side. About 1 minute before chicken is done, grill or broil split sides of rolls until golden. Just before chicken is done, drape chicken with chiles and top with cheese; remove from grill or broiler as soon as cheese has melted. Stir together mayonnaise and cilantro and spread onto split sides of all roll halves. Place chicken breasts on bottom halves and top with lettuce, tomato and bun tops. Makes 4 servings.

Chavo

JAXON'S, EL PASO, TEXAS

The most popular sandwich at the popular Jaxon's restaurants is the Chavo—the name derived from its combination of chicken and avocado. I think the sandwich's special appeal could well be attributed to the zesty marinade in which the chicken steeps for up to 24 hours. Thanks for the recipe go to company vice-president Mandy Zabriskie, who suggests serving the sandwiches with ranch-style beans, pineapple-laced cole slaw or curly French fries.

1/4 cup vegetable oil
2 tablespoons lime juice
2 tablespoons finely chopped green onions
1 tablespoon lemon juice
1 tablespoon dry vermouth
1/2 teaspoon dried hot red chile flakes
6 boneless, skinless chicken breasts
6 kaiser rolls, split
3 tablespoons unsalted butter, softened
3 tablespoons mayonnaise
12 bacon strips, cooked
1 large ripe Haas avocado, cut lengthwise into 12 slices
6 large firm, ripe tomato slices
6 lettuce leaves

In a glass or ceramic bowl, stir together oil, lime juice, green onions, lemon juice, vermouth and chile flakes. Turn chicken breasts in mixture to coat, cover with plastic wrap and marinate in refrigerator 12 to 24 hours. Preheat grill or broiler until very hot. Grill chicken breasts just until no longer pink in the center, about 5 minutes per side, taking care not to overcook. Meanwhile, butter split sides of rolls and toast on grill or under broiler until golden. Spread mayonnaise on bottom halves of rolls. Place chicken on top. Then arrange bacon, avocado, tomato and lettuce on each chicken breast and top with other roll halves. Makes 6 servings.

Chicken, Bell Pepper & Watercress Medley with Lemon-Pepper Mayonnaise

This casual, quickly prepared sandwich combines strips of grilled chicken and roasted red bell pepper with crisp, peppery watercress leaves and a fresh-tasting mayonnaise. Pita breads are the best vehicles for the tossed assemblage.

3 tablespoons olive oil
1/4 cup lemon juice
1 teaspoon dried leaf rosemary
1-1/2 pounds boneless, skinless chicken breasts
Salt and pepper
6 tablespoons mayonnaise
2 medium-size red bell peppers, roasted, stemmed, seeded and peeled (page 2) and
    torn into thin strips, juices reserved
4 individual-size pita breads
1 cup packed watercress leaves, torn into bite-size pieces

In a shallow bowl, stir together oil, half the lemon juice and rosemary. Turn chicken breasts in mixture and marinate at room temperature about 15 minutes. Preheat grill or broiler until very hot. Remove chicken from marinade. Season chicken with salt and pepper and grill or broil close to heat until no longer pink in center, 4 to 5 minutes per side, basting with marinade. Meanwhile, in a small bowl, stir together mayonnaise, remaining lemon juice and pepper juices. When chicken is done, set aside and grill or broil pita breads until lightly golden but still soft, about 30 seconds per side. Cut breads into halves and spread insides generously with mayonnaise. Cut chicken crosswise into 1/2-inch-wide strips and toss with bell pepper and watercress. Stuff into pita halves. Makes 4 servings.

Spicy Chicken Sandwich with Jicama & Hoisin Mayonnaise

PETER DOWER, ANNA'S CAFE, PHOENIX, ARIZONA

Fresh, healthy and innovative food is the specialty of Anna's Cafe, one of the best little lunch spots in Phoenix. This sandwich, one of owner/chef Peter Dower's most popular offerings, makes good use of economical dark-meat chicken, marinated with readily available Asian seasonings and combined with crunchy jicama. He recommends using red chile over green in the marinade, and suggests you can cut the chile by half if you prefer it less spicy.

1 tablespoon Chinese light soy sauce
1 tablespoon Chinese black vinegar
1 tablespoon dark brown sugar
1 teaspoon finely chopped fresh garlic
1 tablespoon finely chopped and seeded (page 2) fresh red or green chile
1 pound boneless, skinless chicken thigh pieces
1 cup mayonnaise
1/2 tablespoon Chinese hoisin sauce
8 crusty whole-wheat bread slices
4 red-leaf lettuce leaves
1/2 cup thinly shredded jicama
2 very thin red onion slices, separated into rings

In a glass or ceramic dish just large enough to hold the chicken, stir together soy sauce, vinegar, sugar, garlic and chile. Add chicken and marinate—preferably overnight but for at least 3 to 4 hours. Preheat grill or broiler until very hot. Grill chicken just until no longer pink in center, 3 to 4 minutes per side. Meanwhile, in a small bowl, stir together mayonnaise and hoisin. Spread on one side of each bread slice. Place a lettuce leaf on 4 slices and top with jicama. Place grilled chicken on top of jicama and top with onion slices and remaining bread. Cut sandwiches in halves and serve. Makes 4 servings.

Smoked Chicken with Smoked Tomato Salsa, Avocado & Papaya

DAVID JARVIS, MELANGE, NORTHFIELD, ILLINOIS

Chef David Jarvis's tortilla-based contribution suggests the deftly eclectic touch he brings to his menu. You'll find smoked chicken breasts in good-quality gourmet delicatessens.

Smoked Tomato Salsa (see below)
8 ounces skinless smoked chicken breast, chilled and cut or torn into julienne strips
1 ripe but firm Haas avocado, cut into small dice
1 ripe but firm papaya, cut into small dice
1 head Boston lettuce, leaves separated, washed, dried and cut into julienne strips
Juice of 1 lime
3 (6-inch) corn tortillas

Smoked Tomato Salsa

8 plum tomatoes
1 jalapeño pepper, stemmed and seeded (page 2)
1 dried ancho chile, soaked in water to cover until soft
1 garlic clove, peeled
1 teaspoon coarsely chopped red onion
2 teaspoons finely chopped fresh cilantro leaves

Prepare salsa. Preheat oven to 300°F (150°C). In a medium-size bowl, combine chicken, avocado, papaya and lettuce. Add lime juice and gently toss. Put tortillas in oven and heat just until warmed through, 2 to 3 minutes. With a knife, cut tortillas into 4 wedges each. Mound chicken mixture on half the wedges, spoon on salsa and top with remaining wedges. Makes 4 servings.

Smoked Tomato Salsa

Prepare a smoker, following manufacturer's directions. Or make a simple smoker by putting a small barbecue or a large, heavy old pot in a clear area outdoors and lighting charcoal briquets in it. While coals are heating, soak a handful of mesquite chips in cold water. Line a metal rack with heavy-duty foil and punch a few holes in it. Place all ingredients except cilantro on top of rack. When coals have almost completely burned down but are still hot, drain mesquite chips well and scatter over coals; spray with water if they catch fire. Place rack with ingredients at least 8 inches above chips, cover loosely with smoker top or a pot lid and smoke 10 minutes. Remove ingredients and let cool. Put ingredients in a blender, add cilantro and puree. Transfer to a bowl, cover and chill in refrigerator before use.

Diner-Style Ground Chicken Burgers

*Ground chicken, widely available in supermarkets today, offers a healthier
alternative to ground beef in this interpretation of a favorite multilayered burger.
Feel free to substitute ground turkey—or, for that matter, ground beef! If you
can't find a bakery that makes unsliced buns, buy presliced ones and use a bread
knife to cut a third slice from whichever bun half is thicker. And feel free to
elaborate the toppings with your favorite mustard or ketchup.*

1-1/4 pounds ground chicken
1 small brown onion, very finely chopped
Salt and white pepper
4 unsliced hamburger buns
1/4 cup unsalted butter, softened
6 ounces mild Cheddar or American cheese, thinly sliced
1/2 cup bottled thousand island dressing
3/4 cup very thinly shredded iceberg lettuce
12 dill pickle chips

In a medium-size bowl, use your hands to combine chicken and onion. Shape mixture
into 8 equal patties the diameter of the buns. Spray a large heavy skillet or griddle with
nonstick spray and heat over medium to high heat. Season burgers with salt and pepper
and cook until no longer pink in center, 2 to 3 minutes per side. Meanwhile, with a bread
knife, cut each bun into 3 equal slices and spread cut sides with butter. As soon as
burgers are done, drape with cheese, remove from cooking surface and keep warm. Place
sliced buns cut-sides down on cooking surface and cook until lightly browned, about 30
seconds. Spread bottom slices with thousand island dressing, scatter half the lettuce on
top and place a patty on top of lettuce. Spread more dressing on both sides of middle
slices, place on sandwiches and top with remaining lettuce, remaining patties and
pickle chips. Spread remaining dressing on cut sides of top slices and place on sandwiches. Makes 4 servings.

Waldorf-Style Chicken Salad on Croissants with Gruyere & Watercress

Inspired by the recipe originally created a century ago by chef Oscar Tschirky of New York's Waldorf, these sandwiches hold a mayonnaise-bound mixture of chicken meat, apples, celery and walnuts. Use leftover chicken, or cook some expressly for the sandwiches a day in advance. While I'm personally not a great fan of sandwiches served in croissants, those light, buttery, crescent-shaped breakfast rolls make ideal containers for the mixture.

2 cups coarsely chopped cooked chicken meat, preferably white meat
3/4 cup peeled, coarsely chopped apple
1/2 cup thinly sliced celery
1/2 cup coarsely chopped walnuts
1/4 cup golden seedless raisins
2 tablespoons finely chopped fresh chives
3/4 cup mayonnaise
2 tablespoons lemon juice
6 ounces Gruyere or Emmenthal cheese, thinly sliced
1-1/2 cups watercress leaves
4 large croissants, split

In a medium-size bowl, toss together chicken, apple, celery, walnuts, raisins and chives. Add mayonnaise and lemon juice and stir until thoroughly mixed. Drape cheese on bottom halves of croissants and arrange watercress on top, decoratively overlapping edges. Spoon salad mixture over watercress and place remaining croissant halves on top. Makes 4 servings.

Chinese Chicken Salad Sandwiches

A variation on the popular luncheon salad, these sandwiches
contain an appealing combination of colors, tastes and textures.
It's worth cooking up some chicken breasts fresh for the sandwiches,
though you can certainly use leftovers if you like.

2 cups thinly sliced cooked chicken, preferably white meat
3/4 cup well-drained Mandarin orange segments
3/4 cup roasted whole small cashews
1/4 cup finely chopped fresh cilantro
2 small green onions, thinly sliced
1 red bell pepper, cut into 1/4- to 1/2-inch dice
3/4 cup mayonnaise
1 tablespoon lemon juice
2 teaspoons sesame oil
8 raisin pumpernickel, whole-wheat or multi-grain bread slices
1 cup alfalfa or mustard sprouts

In a medium-size bowl, toss together chicken, Mandarin oranges, cashews, cilantro, green onions and bell pepper. Add mayonnaise, lemon juice and sesame oil and stir until well combined. Spread salad mixture on half the bread slices, then top with sprouts and remaining bread. Cut into halves. Makes 4 servings.

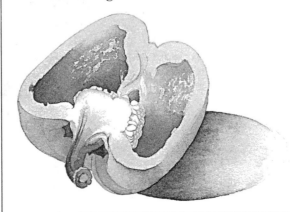

Charred Turkey Steak with Balsamic-Grilled Mushroom Caps

Generous steak-like slices of uncooked turkey breast are usually available at supermarket meat counters; ask your butcher for them if you don't see any.

1/2 cup olive oil
1 tablespoon lemon juice
2 pounds turkey breast, cut into large 1/2-inch-thick steaks
2 tablespoons balsamic vinegar
12 large cultivated mushrooms, stems removed and discarded
Salt
Freshly ground pepper
8 large sourdough bread slices
Mayonnaise
Creamy Dijon-style mustard
1 cup arugula leaves, or 8 radicchio leaves

In a shallow bowl, stir together 3 tablespoons olive oil and lemon juice; turn turkey slices in mixture to coat. In another bowl, stir together 3 more tablespoons oil and balsamic vinegar; turn mushroom caps in mixture to coat. Leave turkey and mushrooms to marinate about 30 minutes at room temperature. Meanwhile, preheat grill or broiler until very hot. Season turkey with salt and pepper and grill close to heat until browned on both sides and just cooked through, about 3 minutes per side. After turning turkey over, brush bread with remaining oil and season mushrooms with salt and pepper; put both on grill, cooking until mushrooms are golden and bread is toasted, 30 to 60 seconds per side. Spread one side of half the bread slices to taste with mayonnaise, the others with mustard. Place turkey steaks on half the slices and top with grilled mushrooms, arugula or radicchio and remaining bread. Cut into halves. Makes 4 servings.

Peppered Turkey Burgers with Cranberry Sauce

*Like Thanksgiving on a bun, these easy-to-make burgers deliver
the best flavors of the holiday season year round.*

2 pounds ground turkey
1 medium-size onion, coarsely chopped
1 teaspoon dried leaf sage, crumbled
Salt
Whole black peppercorns
1 (1-lb.) can jellied cranberry sauce
6 tablespoons mayonnaise
2 tablespoons coarse-grained Dijon-style mustard
4 large hamburger buns

In a medium-size bowl, stir together turkey, onion and sage. With your hands, form mixture into 4 equal patties slightly larger than diameters of buns. Season with salt on both sides. Put peppercorns in a pepper grinder and adjust grinder to coarsest setting—usually achieved by loosening bolt at top of grinder. Grind pepper generously over both sides of burgers and gently pat into surfaces. Preheat grill or broiler until very hot. Cook turkey burgers until no longer pink in center, 4 to 5 minutes per side. Meanwhile, open both ends of cranberry sauce can and use one end to push sauce out of can in a single cylinder. With a knife, cut 4 circular slices of sauce, each about 1/2 inch thick; reserve remaining sauce for another use. In a small bowl, stir together mayonnaise and mustard. Spread both halves of each bun with mustard-mayonnaise to taste, place burgers on bottom halves and top with cranberry sauce and bun tops. Makes 4 servings.

Oven-Roasted Turkey with Hummus & Feta Cheese

The satisfyingly earthy flavor of the Middle-Eastern garbanzo-and-sesame puree known as hummus enriches and moistens these stuffed pita sandwiches. Most good ethnic delis, and some supermarkets as well, offer freshly made hummus.

Hummus (see below)
4 individual-size whole-wheat or white pita breads
1-1/2 pounds roast turkey breast, cut into moderately thin slices
6 ounces feta cheese
1/2 cup pitted black Mediterranean-style olives
2 large Roma tomatoes, thinly sliced
1 cup alfalfa sprouts

Hummus

1 cup canned garbanzo beans, well drained
1 medium-size garlic clove, peeled
3 tablespoons tahini (Middle Eastern sesame paste)
2 tablespoons lemon juice
1 tablespoon olive oil
Salt and white pepper

Prepare Hummus. Preheat oven to 400°F (205°C). Put pita breads in oven to warm through, 2 to 3 minutes. With a bread knife, cut pitas into halves. Carefully open cut sides and spread Hummus generously inside pockets on both sides. Divide turkey, cheese, olives and tomatoes among pita halves. Garnish with sprouts. Makes 4 servings.

Hummus

Put garbanzos, garlic, tahini, lemon juice and olive oil in a food processor with the metal blade. Process until pureed. Season to taste with salt and pepper. Transfer to a bowl, cover with plastic wrap and refrigerate until using.

Southwestern Reuben

FREDERICK KING, RENNICK'S RESTAURANT, PHOENIX AIRPORT HILTON, PHOENIX, ARIZONA

Award-winning Executive Chef Frederick King brings innovative flair to his dining room close by Sky Harbor Airport. He uses his own mesquite-smoked turkey breast for these sandwiches, which he suggests serving with spicy-seasoned French fries. Good-quality smoked turkey breast, mesquite or not, is widely available at delis and supermarkets. Jicama, the crisp, refreshing root vegetable that is a favorite of Southwestern cooking, may also be found in most well-stocked produce sections.

1/4 pound unsalted butter
1/2 pound jicama, peeled and cut into julienne strips
8 sourdough bread slices
8 (1-oz.) pepper Monterey Jack cheese slices
1 pound thinly sliced smoked turkey breast

In a large skillet, melt half the butter over medium heat; melt remaining butter over medium heat in another large skillet or on a griddle. Sauté jicama in first skillet until tender and golden, 3 to 5 minutes. Meanwhile, place bread slices side-by-side in other skillet or on griddle and place 1 slice of cheese on each; cook until undersides are golden-brown, about 3 minutes. Add turkey to jicama and continue sautéing just until heated through. Pile turkey and jicama on top of cheese on half the bread slices and top with remaining slices. Cut diagonally. Makes 4 servings.

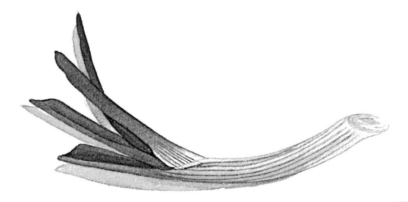

Italian Turkey with Pickled Artichoke Hearts

*The sharp flavor and al dente texture of pickled artichoke
hearts casts the taste of roast turkey breast in sharp relief
in these sandwiches reminiscent of a Tuscan picnic.*

8 thick slices crusty Italian sourdough or white bread
2 tablespoons unsalted butter, softened
2 tablespoons mayonnaise
1 tablespoon Italian-style mustard
1-1/2 pounds roast turkey breast, thickly sliced
1 cup pickled Italian-style artichoke hearts, well drained
4 large leaves radicchio or red-leaf lettuce

Spread one side of half the bread slices with butter. In a small bowl, stir together mayonnaise and mustard and spread on remaining bread slices. Arrange turkey evenly on buttered bread. In a small bowl, coarsely mash artichoke hearts with a fork, then spread on top of turkey. Top with radicchio or lettuce and remaining bread and cut into halves. Makes 4 servings.

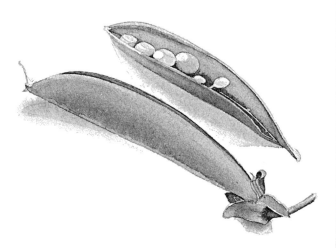

Turkey & Mushroom Melts

Quickly sautéed mushrooms elaborate these turkey variations on deli favorites.

1/2 cup unsalted butter
2 tablespoons vegetable oil
1/2 pound cultivated mushrooms, cut into 1/4-inch-thick slices
1 teaspoon lemon juice
1/4 teaspoon salt
1/4 teaspoon pepper
8 sourdough or rye bread slices
1/2 pound Swiss, Gruyere or Emmenthaler cheese, coarsely shredded
1 pound thinly sliced roast turkey breast

In a large skillet, heat 2 tablespoons butter with oil over medium to high heat. Add mushrooms and sauté, stirring rapidly, until edges turn golden, about 5 minutes. Sprinkle with lemon juice, season with salt and pepper, remove from skillet and set aside. Spread remaining butter evenly on one side of each bread slice. Turn slices buttered sides down. Sprinkle about a quarter of the cheese in even layers on top of 4 bread slices. Evenly layer half of turkey on top. Sprinkle another quarter of cheese over turkey and top with an even layer of mushrooms. Add another quarter of cheese, remaining turkey and remaining cheese, finishing with remaining bread slices placed buttered sides up. Spray a large, heavy skillet with nonstick cooking spray and heat over medium heat. Add sandwiches and fry, pressing down frequently and firmly with the back of a spatula, until undersides are golden-brown, 3 to 4 minutes. Carefully turn sandwiches over and fry, pressing frequently, 3 to 4 minutes more. Cut into halves and serve. Makes 4 servings.

Smoked Turkey with Smoked Gouda, Radicchio & Sun-Dried Tomato Mayonnaise

Though freshly sliced smoked turkey from a good delicatessen is preferable, these sandwiches are still excellent made with the prepackaged smoked turkey breast widely available in supermarket refrigerator cases. A good, flavorful, dense-textured bread will stand up best to the strong tastes in the filling.

8 rye or pumpernickel bread slices
Sun-Dried Tomato Mayonnaise (page 33)
1 pound thinly sliced smoked turkey breast
2 Roma tomatoes, thinly sliced
1/2 pound thinly sliced smoked Gouda cheese
1 cup shredded radicchio leaves

Spread one side of each bread slice with Sun-Dried Tomato Mayonnaise. Arrange turkey evenly on half the slices. Top with tomatoes, cheese, radicchio and remaining bread. Cut into halves. Makes 4 servings.

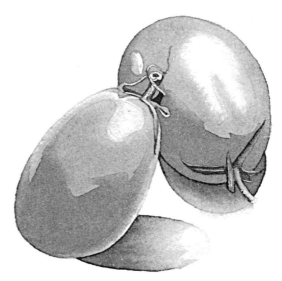

Turkey & Avocado Sandwich

KATHLEEN TURNER, OK CAFE, ATLANTA, GEORGIA

As this lavish version of a turkey club suggests, outstanding examples of traditional Southern-style diner food reign supreme at Kathleen Turner's 24-hour-a-day cafe in Atlanta. She serves it with potato chips and dill pickle spears.

8 white, whole-wheat, rye or sourdough bread slices
1/4 cup mayonnaise
1 pound sliced cooked turkey
1 ripe Hass avocado, cut lengthwise into 12 slices
3/4 cup alfalfa sprouts
8 bacon slices, crisp-cooked
4 medium-size romaine lettuce leaves
8 thin firm, ripe tomato slices
8 pimento-stuffed olives

Evenly spread one side of each bread slice with mayonnaise. Neatly stack turkey on half the slices. On top of turkey, evenly layer avocado, sprouts, bacon, lettuce and tomato, in that order. Top with remaining bread. Spear each olive on a frilly wooden pick and push 2 picks through each sandwich near opposite corners. Cut each sandwich diagonally into halves, between picks. Makes 4 servings.

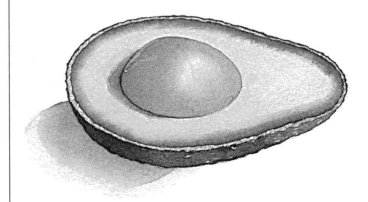

Turkey Salad Sandwiches with Fresh Cranberries

*A great way to liven up the scraps of meat from a holiday turkey,
the filling for these sandwiches includes tangy fresh cranberries.*

1/2 cup fresh cranberries
1/4 cup sugar
2 tablespoons orange juice
1 tablespoon grated orange zest
2 cups coarsely chopped cooked turkey meat
1/4 cup slivered almonds
2 tablespoons finely chopped Italian parsley
2 green onions, thinly sliced
3/4 cup mayonnaise
4 whole-wheat or multi-grain sandwich rolls, split
4 large red-leaf lettuce leaves

In a food processor with the metal blade, process cranberries with sugar, orange juice and zest, using on-off pulses until coarsely chopped. Transfer to a bowl, cover with plastic wrap and refrigerate 3 to 4 hours. Before serving, toss cranberry mixture with turkey, almonds, parsley and green onions. Add mayonnaise and stir until combined. Spoon mixture onto sandwich rolls and top with lettuce. Makes 4 servings.

Seafood Sandwiches

How fortunate that the growing interest in the sandwich's culinary merits coincides with a dramatic increase in the amount of seafood we all consume.

The sandwiches in this chapter are very much the product of that happy fact. Tuna, salmon, swordfish, snapper, codfish, catfish, shrimp, crab, lobster and oysters: Each of these popular varieties of seafood stars here—some in several different guises. And, while most exemplify the lighter approach to eating so popular today, there is no lack of flavor or satisfaction.

Nor do you necessarily need an outstanding fish market near your home to test these recipe-rich waters: Just open a can of tuna or salmon and a generous catch of sandwiches awaits your enjoyment!

Yellowfin Tuna Burgers with Ginger-Mustard Glaze

MICHAEL ROMANO, UNION SQUARE CAFE, NEW YORK, NEW YORK

Danny Meyer's three-star-winning Union Square Cafe quickly became a Manhattan institution after opening in 1985. In recent years, it has gained even greater acclaim for the trend-setting cuisine of chef Michael Romano, a native New Yorker trained in some of Europe's finest kitchens. His recipe complements the texture and flavor of fresh tuna with a mixture of French and Asian seasonings.

Ginger-Mustard Glaze (see below)
3 pounds fresh yellowfin tuna, well-trimmed
1 tablespoon finely chopped garlic
1 tablespoon Dijon-style mustard
1 tablespoon red (cayenne) pepper
Salt and pepper
1/4 cup light olive oil
6 egg-bread rolls or other soft rolls, split
3 tablespoons unsalted butter, softened

Ginger-Mustard Glaze

1/2 cup teriyaki sauce
1/2 cup good-quality veal or chicken stock
2 tablespoons Champagne vinegar
2 tablespoons honey
1 tablespoon Dijon-style mustard
1/2 tablespoon finely chopped gingerroot
1/2 teaspoon finely chopped garlic

Prepare Ginger-Mustard Glaze. With a large, sharp knife, chop tuna by hand to consistency of hamburger; carefully remove all traces of sinew from chopped tuna. In a medium-size bowl, mix tuna with garlic, mustard, cayenne, salt and pepper. Shape into 6 burgers sized to fit rolls. Preheat broiler until very hot. In a large skillet, heat oil over

medium-high heat and sauté burgers until nicely browned but still rare inside, 1 to 1-1/2 minutes per side; alternatively, lightly brush burgers with oil and grill or broil. While burgers cook, lightly spread split sides of rolls with butter and toast under broiler. Place burgers on bottom halves of rolls, spread Ginger-Mustard Glaze on top and cover with top halves. Makes 6 servings.

Ginger-Mustard Glaze

In a saucepan, combine all ingredients. Bring to a boil over high heat. Then reduce heat and simmer briskly, stirring frequently, until mixture reduces to a consistency thick enough to coat the back of a wooden spoon, about 5 minutes. Pour through a fine sieve into a bowl before using.

Seared Ahi Tuna with Pickled Ginger & Wasabi Mayonnaise

Japanese sushi inspired this lively tasting sandwich. Use the absolutely freshest, best-quality ahi or other kind of tuna you can find. With the popularity of Japanese cuisine today, the accompanying ingredients are easy to find in well-stocked supermarkets or Asian markets.

2 tablespoons peanut oil
2 tablespoons rice wine vinegar
2 tablespoons soy sauce
1 teaspoon sesame oil
4 ahi tuna fillets, about 6 ounces each and no more than 1 inch thick
8 sourdough bread slices
1 tablespoon lemon juice
1/2 teaspoon wasabi (green horseradish) powder
6 tablespoons mayonnaise
1 small Japanese cucumber, cut crosswise into slices
1/4 cup pink Japanese-style pickled ginger, cut into julienne strips
1/4 cup mustard or radish sprouts

In a shallow bowl, stir together peanut oil, vinegar, soy sauce and sesame oil. Turn tuna fillets in mixture and leave at room temperature to marinate about 30 minutes. Meanwhile, preheat grill or broiler until very hot. Remove tuna from marinade and cook very close to heat until well seared but still pink in middle, 1 to 2 minutes per side. Meanwhile, toast bread until golden in a toaster, on grill or under broiler. In a medium-size bowl, stir together lemon juice and wasabi to make a thin paste; then stir in mayonnaise until well blended. Spread to taste on one side of each piece of toast. Place tuna on half the toast pieces. Arrange cucumbers on top, scatter with ginger and sprouts and top with remaining bread. Cut into halves. Makes 4 servings.

Fresh Ahi Tuna Salad with Maui-Onion Remoulade

*If you're planning to grill tuna for dinner, buy and cook some extra
so you can make this elegant version of a mayonnaise-based tuna salad.*

2 tablespoons each olive oil and lemon juice
1/2 tablespoon finely chopped fresh dill
1-1/2 pounds fresh ahi tuna fillets
Maui-Onion Remoulade (see below)
Salt and white pepper
8 good-quality crusty French bread slices
1/4 cup unsalted butter, softened
4 butter lettuce or red-leaf lettuce leaves

Maui-Onion Remoulade

1/2 cup mayonnaise
2-1/2 tablespoons finely chopped Maui, Vidalia, Walla Walla or sweet red onion
1 tablespoon finely chopped sour dill-pickled gherkin
1 tablespoon finely chopped Italian parsley
1/2 tablespoon finely grated lemon zest
1 teaspoon lemon juice

In a shallow bowl, stir together olive oil, lemon juice and dill. Turn tuna in mixture; marinate at room temperature 15 to 30 minutes. Prepare remoulade. Preheat grill or broiler until very hot. Season tuna with salt and pepper and grill close to heat just until cooked through, 3 to 4 minutes per side. Cool to room temperature; cover and refrigerate until cold. With your fingertips break tuna into 1/4-inch-thick flakes. In a medium-size bowl, toss tuna lightly with remoulade. Spread one side of each bread slice with butter and arrange tuna salad on top of half the slices. Top with lettuce and remaining bread. Makes 4 servings.

Maui-Onion Remoulade

In a small bowl, stir together all ingredients. Cover and refrigerate until ready to use.

Italian Tuna Salad on Focaccia

If a local bakery has focaccia, serve this light, zesty tuna salad on it. Alternatively, use a good-quality sourdough or other coarse, dense-crumbed country-style bread.

3 (6-1/2-oz.) cans Italian-style light tuna in olive oil, drained, oil reserved
3 tablespoons finely chopped red onion
2 tablespoons small capers, drained
1-1/2 tablespoons finely chopped Italian parsley
1 tablespoon lemon juice
Pepper
8 (6-inch) squares Italian-style focaccia, or 8 sourdough bread slices
1/4 cup mayonnaise
4 butter lettuce leaves

In a medium-size bowl, use a fork to toss together tuna, onion, capers, parsley and lemon juice, coarsely breaking up tuna. Add enough reserved oil to coat mixture lightly and season to taste with pepper. Lightly spread one side of each piece of bread with mayonnaise. Spoon tuna mixture evenly over half the pieces. Top with lettuce and remaining bread. Cut diagonally into halves. Makes 4 servings.

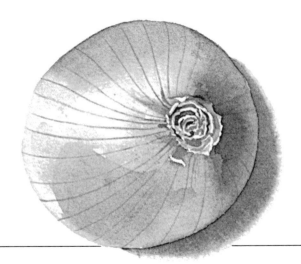

Hot Tuna Grinder

My own interpretation of a sandwich that is legendary among present and former Yalies, who flock to eat the version served at Broadway Pizza in New Haven. Serve with peperoncini—Italian pickled peppers.

3 (6-1/2-oz.) cans water-packed tuna, drained
1 cup mayonnaise
2 tablespoons lemon juice
1 tablespoon finely chopped Italian parsley
1 tablespoon finely chopped fresh chives
1 teaspoon dried celery seed
Salt and pepper
4 long Italian rolls, about 8 inches each
3/4 pound thinly sliced provolone cheese
2 tablespoons balsamic vinegar
1/2 tablespoon dried leaf oregano
2 tablespoons olive oil
1-1/2 cups very finely shredded iceberg lettuce, well chilled

Preheat oven to 500°F (260°C). In a medium-size bowl, use a fork to mash together tuna, mayonnaise, lemon juice, parsley, chives and celery seed until well blended and very smooth. Season to taste with salt and pepper. With a bread knife, split rolls lengthwise without cutting all the way through; open out rolls flat. Spread tuna mixture along one side of each roll. Drape cheese over tuna, transfer to a baking sheet and bake until cheese melts, 5 to 7 minutes. Meanwhile, in a small bowl stir together vinegar, oregano and salt and pepper to taste, then briskly stir in oil. Arrange lettuce on top of tuna and cheese and drizzle with oil-and-vinegar dressing. Close rolls and cut into halves. Makes 4 servings.

Grilled Salmon Sandwich with Tapenade

The Provençal black-olive-and-anchovy spread known as tapenade provides contrast and enhancement for the rich, sweet taste of grilled salmon in this wonderfully aromatic sandwich. Be sure to buy good brine-cured olives—the kind sold in gourmet delicatessens and Italian markets.

Tapenade (see below)
1/4 cup olive oil
2 tablespoons lemon juice
4 skinless, boneless salmon fillets, about 6 ounces each
Salt and white pepper
8 sourdough bread slices
1/4 cup mayonnaise
2 large Roma tomatoes, thinly sliced
1 cup packed watercress leaves, torn into bite-size pieces

Tapenade

1/2 cup pitted brine-cured ripe olives
2 tablespoons olive oil
1 tablespoon capers, drained
1 tablespoon coarsely torn fresh Italian parsley leaves
2 teaspoons lemon juice
2 anchovy fillets, drained
1 medium to large garlic clove, peeled

Prepare Tapenade. In a shallow bowl, stir together 2 tablespoons olive oil and the lemon juice. Turn salmon fillets in mixture and marinate at room temperature 30 minutes. Preheat grill or broiler until very hot. Season salmon with salt and pepper and grill until golden-brown but still slightly translucent in center, 4 to 5 minutes per side. After turning salmon, brush bread on both sides with remaining oil and grill until golden-brown, about 1 minute per side. Spread mayonnaise on one side of each bread slice. Place

salmon fillets on top of half the slices and spoon Tapenade generously over salmon; top with tomato slices, watercress and remaining bread. Cut into halves or leave whole. Makes 4 servings.

Tapenade

Put all ingredients in a food processor fitted with the metal blade. Pulse processor a few times to coarsely chop, then run continuously, stopping several times to scrape down bowl, until pureed to a smooth paste.

Grilled Salmon B.L.T.

GERRY KLASKALA, BUCKHEAD DINER, ATLANTA, GEORGIA

This sandwich is typical of the elegant, contemporary approach Buckhead Diner chef and managing partner Gerry Klaskala takes to traditional diner fare.

Tarragon Mayonnaise (see below)
4 skinless, boneless salmon fillets, about 1/4 pound each
4 teaspoons olive oil
Salt and freshly ground pepper
8 brioche or challah bread slices, 1/2 inch thick
1 cup finely shredded lettuce
2 tomatoes, thinly sliced
8 bacon strips, crisp-cooked

Tarragon Mayonnaise

2/3 cup mayonnaise
1/2 tablespoon lemon juice
1 teaspoon finely chopped fresh tarragon
1 shallot, finely chopped
Salt and freshly ground pepper

Prepare mayonnaise. Preheat grill or broiler until medium-hot. Lightly brush salmon on both sides with oil and season to taste with salt and pepper. Grill or broil until slightly translucent in center, 2 to 3 minutes per side. Meanwhile, toast brioche and generously spread mayonnaise on one side of each slice. Top 4 slices with lettuce and tomato. Place grilled salmon on top, then bacon. Cut remaining slices diagonally into halves and prop 2 triangles against either side of each sandwich. Makes 4 servings.

Tarragon Mayonnaise

In a small bowl, stir together mayonnaise, lemon juice, tarragon and shallot. Season to taste with salt and pepper. Makes about 3/4 cup.

Southwestern Cumin-Crusted Salmon with Cilantro Pesto

The heady aromas of the Southwest pervade this robust sandwich.

1/4 cup olive oil
2 tablespoons lemon juice
1 tablespoon whole cumin seeds
4 skinless, boneless salmon fillets, about 6 ounces each
Salt and white pepper
8 sourdough bread slices
1/4 cup mayonnaise
Cilantro Pesto (see below)
4 whole canned roasted mild green chiles, cut open

Cilantro Pesto

1/3 cup packed fresh cilantro leaves
1/4 cup grated Parmesan cheese
1/4 cup pine nuts, toasted (page 3)
1/4 cup olive oil
1 medium-size garlic clove, peeled

In a shallow bowl, stir together 2 tablespoons olive oil, the lemon juice and cumin seeds. Turn salmon fillets in mixture, evenly coating their surfaces with the seeds, and marinate at room temperature 30 minutes. Preheat grill or broiler until very hot. Season salmon with salt and pepper and grill until golden-brown but still slightly translucent in center, 4 to 5 minutes per side. After turning salmon, brush bread on both sides with remaining oil and grill until golden-brown, about 1 minute per side. Spread mayonnaise on one side of each bread slice. Place salmon fillets on top of half the slices and spoon pesto generously over salmon; top with whole chiles and remaining bread. Cut into halves or leave whole. Makes 4 servings.

Cilantro Pesto

Put all ingredients in a food processor fitted with the metal blade. Pulse to coarsely chop, then run continuously, stopping to scrape down bowl, until a smooth paste.

Grilled Salmon, Mizuni & Papaya Sandwich

JIMMY SCHMIDT, THE RATTLESNAKE CLUB, DETROIT, MICHIGAN

A native Midwesterner professionally trained in France, Jimmy Schmidt has, since 1977, enjoyed an ever-greater reputation as one of Detroit's—and America's—most innovative and enterprising chefs. His masterly grasp of classic techniques and fast-breaking trends is well-evident in this sandwich, which intriguingly combines tropical, European, Asian and American influences. Rich and spicy little mizuni leaves, a popular ingredient in Japanese cooking, are available in Asian markets and well-stocked greengrocers. Schmidt suggests baby mustard greens as a substitute.

Papaya-Mustard Spread (see below)
Olive or canola oil
1 Vidalia onion or other sweet onion, thickly sliced
4 salmon escalopes, about 3 ounces each
8 high-fiber whole-wheat bread slices, about 1/3 inch thick
2 red bell peppers, roasted, peeled, seeded (page 2) and torn into strips
1 bunch mizuni or baby mustard greens

Papaya-Mustard Spread

1 ripe papaya, seeded (seeds reserved for Toasted Papaya Seeds, see below), peeled and diced
1/4 cup lime juice
2 tablespoons grainy mustard
1/4 cup finely shredded fresh basil
1/4 cup finely chopped fresh chives
1/4 teaspoon freshly ground pepper

Toasted Papaya Seeds

Reserved seeds of fresh papaya

Preheat grill or broiler. Prepare Papaya-Mustard Spread and refrigerate. Toast papaya seeds, if using. With the oil, brush grill (omit this step if using broiler). Place onion slices on grill and cook until tender, 3 to 5 minutes per side. Set aside. Place salmon escalopes on grill and cook until underside is well-seared, about 3 minutes; turn over and cook until done, about 2 minutes more. Spread bread slices with Papaya-Mustard Spread and, if you like, sprinkle with Toasted Papaya Seeds. Evenly distribute grilled onions and roasted peppers on 4 slices. Top with salmon, then mizuni leaves. Place remaining bread slices on top. Makes 4 servings.

Papaya-Mustard Spread

In a food processor fitted with the metal blade, put papaya, lime juice and mustard. Process until smoothly pureed. Add basil, chives and pepper and pulse briefly just to combine. Cover and refrigerate until serving. Makes about 1-1/2 cups.

Toasted Papaya Seeds

Preheat oven to 300°F (150°C). Put papaya seeds in a strainer and rub with the back of a wooden spoon or spatula to loosen the gelatinous outer seed coverings. Rinse well under cold running water until clean. Spread on a baking sheet and toast in oven until crisp and crunchy, 7 to 10 minutes.

Classic Smoked Salmon Sandwiches

*Buy the best-quality smoked salmon you can find for this classic
open-faced presentation. Make them up fresh just before serving.*

8 thin slices good-quality black or brown bread
1/4 cup unsalted butter, softened
1/2 small red onion, very finely chopped
3/4 pound thinly sliced smoked salmon
2 hard-boiled eggs, whites finely chopped, yolks finely grated or sieved
1 tablespoon small capers, drained
1 tablespoon finely chopped fresh chives
2 lemons, cut into 4 wedges each
Freshly ground pepper

Spread one side of each bread slice with butter. Scatter onion over butter and top neatly with salmon. With a sharp knife, cut slices diagonally in halves. Decoratively garnish each triangle with egg whites and yolks, capers and chives. Serve with lemon wedges and a pepper mill for guests to individually season their portions. Makes 4 servings.

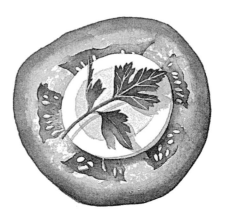

Salmon Salad with Crisp Cucumber on Brown Bread

*Simple though it is, there's something especially lavish
about making these old-fashioned sandwiches. All the better to
know that canned salmon is particularly rich in calcium.*

1 medium-size Japanese or regular cucumber
2 (7-1/2-ounce) cans pink salmon, drained
2 hard-boiled eggs, coarsely chopped
1/4 cup mayonnaise
2 tablespoons lemon juice
2 teaspoons finely chopped fresh dill, or 1 teaspoon dried dill weed
3 tablespoons unsalted butter, softened
4 thick slices whole-wheat or brown bread

Leave Japanese cucumber unpeeled and unseeded; peel regular cucumber, halve lengthwise and, with a teaspoon, scoop out seeds. Cut cucumber crosswise into 1/4-inch-thick slices and place in a bowl filled with water and ice cubes. Leave to crisp 1/2 hour. In a medium-size bowl, use a fork to stir together salmon, eggs, mayonnaise, lemon juice and dill, breaking salmon into coarse flakes. Drain cucumber and pat dry with kitchen towels. Spread butter on one side of each bread slice and gently press cucumber slices into butter. Spread salmon mixture on half the bread slices and top with remaining bread. Cut diagonally into halves. Makes 4 servings.

Swordfish with Tomatillo-Cilantro Salsa

The meaty taste of swordfish gets a tangy complement from the salsa topping and the grilled sourdough bread. Use the canned tomatillos sold in the specialty foods sections of well-stocked supermarkets or Latin American shops.

6 tablespoons olive oil
2 tablespoons lime juice
4 swordfish fillets, about 6 ounces each, trimmed of skin
1 garlic clove, finely chopped
2 tablespoons finely chopped red onion
1 cup canned tomatillos
1/2 cup dry white wine
1/2 tablespoon sugar
Salt and white pepper
Red (cayenne) pepper
1/4 cup finely chopped fresh cilantro
4 good-quality sourdough bread slices
4 fresh cilantro sprigs, for garnish

In a shallow bowl, stir 2 tablespoons olive oil together with the lime juice. Turn swordfish in mixture and marinate at room temperature about 30 minutes. Meanwhile, in a medium-size saucepan, heat 2 tablespoons more oil over medium heat. Add garlic and onion and sauté until transparent, 2 to 3 minutes. Add tomatillos, wine and sugar, bring to a boil, reduce heat and simmer until thick but still fairly liquid, 7 to 10 minutes; season to taste with salt and white pepper and keep warm. Meanwhile, heat grill or broiler until very hot. Season swordfish to taste with salt and white pepper and lightly dust with cayenne. Cook swordfish close to heat until done but still moist, 3 to 5 minutes per side. Stir chopped cilantro into tomatillo mixture. Brush bread with remaining oil and grill or broil until golden, 30 to 60 seconds per side. Put a bread slice on each plate, top with a swordfish fillet and sauce; garnish with cilantro sprig. Makes 4 servings.

Grilled Swordfish Sandwiches with Roasted Peppers & Citrus Mayonnaise

The natural sweetness of the roasted peppers and citrus-zest-flavored sauce subtly highlight the flavor of the swordfish.

6 tablespoons olive oil
2 tablespoons orange juice
4 swordfish fillets, about 6 ounces each, trimmed of skin
Salt and pepper
8 good-quality sourdough bread slices
6 tablespoons mayonnaise
1 tablespoon finely grated orange zest
1 tablespoon finely grated lemon zest
1 tablespoon finely chopped Italian parsley
1 red bell pepper, roasted, peeled and seeded (page 2) and torn into 1/2-inch-wide strips
1 yellow or green bell pepper, roasted, peeled, stemmed and seeded (page 2) and torn into 1/2-inch-wide strips

In a shallow bowl, stir 2 tablespoons olive oil together with the orange juice. Turn swordfish in mixture and marinate at room temperature about 30 minutes. Heat grill or broiler until very hot. Season swordfish to taste with salt and pepper. Cook swordfish close to heat until done but still moist, 3 to 5 minutes per side. Brush bread with remaining oil and grill or broil until golden, 30 seconds to 1 minute per side. In a small bowl, stir together mayonnaise, citrus zests and parsley. Spread generously on one side of each bread slice. Place swordfish on top of half the bread slices. Drape peppers over fish and top with remaining bread. Cut diagonally into halves. Makes 4 servings.

Red Snapper Burgers with Mango Ketchup

ALLEN SUSSER, CHEF ALLEN'S, AVENTURA, FLORIDA

In North Miami, Allen Susser's restaurant exemplifies the fresh, innovative new American cooking now coming out of Florida. There's a touch of the Caribbean and a touch of Asia in this appealing seafood sandwich. You'll find Thai fish sauce in Asian shops and in the specialty food sections of well-stocked supermarkets.

1/2 cup Mango Ketchup (see below)
1 pound fresh red snapper fillets
3 egg whites
2 tablespoons finely chopped green onion
1 tablespoon Thai fish sauce (nam pla)
1 teaspoon finely chopped fresh dill
1/2 cup dry bread crumbs
1 tablespoon olive oil
8 French bread slices
1/4 pound spinach leaves, thoroughly cleaned and dried

Mango Ketchup

4 medium-size ripe mangos
1/2 cup dry white wine
1/4 cup white vinegar
1/4 cup raw sugar
1 tablespoon ground ginger
1 teaspoon salt
1/2 teaspoon ground allspice
1/2 teaspoon red (cayenne) pepper
1 whole clove
Dash of ground cinnamon

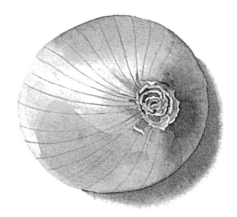

Prepare Mango Ketchup. In a food processor fitted with the metal blade, chop snapper fillets, pulsing the machine and stopping frequently to scrape down the bowl until the fish resembles coarsely ground hamburger. Transfer to a large stainless-steel bowl. Add egg whites, green onion, fish sauce and dill. Mix together, adding enough bread crumbs to bind the mixture. Form by hand into 4 burger shapes about 1-1/2 inches thick; place on a wax paper-lined plate or tray and refrigerate about 1/2 hour. Meanwhile, preheat grill or broiler until very hot. Lightly drizzle olive oil over burgers and grill close to heat just until done, about 1-1/2 minutes per side, taking care not to overcook. Transfer to bread immediately, dress with Mango Ketchup and garnish with spinach leaves. Makes 4 servings.

Mango Ketchup

Peel mango and cut pulp from stone. Put pulp and all other ingredients into a food processor fitted with the metal blade. Pulse until smoothly pureed. Transfer to a heavy saucepan and cook over low heat, stirring frequently, until reduced and thickened, about 1 hour. Remove from heat and let cool to room temperature. Strain through a fine sieve. Transfer to a glass or metal bowl, cover and refrigerate 24 hours before use.

Provençal Club

JEREMIAH TOWER, STARS, SAN FRANCISCO, CALIFORNIA

One of San Francisco's most acclaimed contemporary chefs, Jeremiah Tower makes a traditional seafood preparation from the south of France—brandade, a rich puree of salt cod—the main attraction in his satisfyingly flavorful version of a club sandwich. He suggests serving Nicoise-style cured olives alongside.

Brandade (see below)
8 streaky bacon slices
12 thin slices country-style French bread, 1/8 inch thick
Olive oil
12 tomato slices, 1/8 inch thick
Salt and pepper
1 cup packed arugula leaves

Brandade

1 pound dried salt cod, soaked overnight in cold water and drained
1/2 pound potatoes, peeled and cut into 1-inch chunks
2 garlic cloves, finely chopped
1/2 cup olive oil
Pepper

Prepare Brandade and keep it warm in the top of a double boiler over very low heat. Preheat grill or broiler until very hot. Grill bacon until crisp and golden, 1 to 2 minutes per side; set aside. Lightly brush bread on both sides with oil and grill until crisp and golden on outside but still soft within, 30 seconds to 1 minute per side. Season tomato slices with salt and grill about 30 seconds per side. Spread warm Brandade on 4 bread slices and top with 4 more slices. Place tomato slices on top, season with pepper, then add bacon, arugula and remaining bread. Makes 4 servings.

Brandade

Put soaked and drained salt cod in a medium-size saucepan, cover with cold water and bring to a boil. Drain well, cover with more cold water and bring to a boil again. Remove from heat, cover pan and let cod soak about 15 minutes. Meanwhile, in another saucepan of cold water, cook potatoes over medium to high heat until tender; drain well and set aside. Drain salt cod and remove and discard skin and bones, breaking fish into large flakes. While still warm, put fish, potatoes and garlic in a food processor with the metal blade and pulse machine until finely chopped. With motor running, slowly pour in oil until mixture is thick and creamy. Season to taste with pepper.

Cajun Fried Catfish Po' Boy

DEAN FEARING, THE MANSION ON TURTLE CREEK, DALLAS, TEXAS

*From the acclaimed chef of Dallas' most luxurious hotel comes a sandwich
that presents in elegant fashion the down-home Southern flavor of spicy
fried catfish. Farm-grown fresh catfish is available ever-more-widely at
good-quality fish markets. At The Mansion, they serve the sandwich on their
own-baked black-pepper brioche bread; any bakery-bought brioche or other
rich egg bread would be an acceptable substitute.*

1/4 cup Creole Seasoning (see below)
Jalapeño Tartar Sauce (see following page)
1 cup white wine
2 tablespoons Creole mustard
1 pound baby catfish fillets
1 cup instant flour
1 cup cornstarch
Vegetable oil for deep-frying
8 fresh-baked brioche slices
2 medium-size tomatoes, thinly sliced
4 large lettuce leaves

Creole Seasoning
3 tablespoons medium-hot-to-hot paprika
2 tablespoons salt
1 tablespoon red (cayenne) pepper
1 tablespoon black pepper
1 tablespoon white pepper
1 tablespoon garlic powder
1 tablespoon onion powder
1/2 tablespoon dried leaf basil
1/2 tablespoon dried leaf oregano
1/2 tablespoon dried leaf thyme

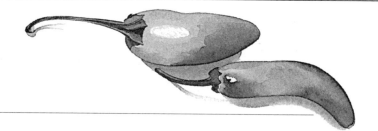

Jalapeño Tartar Sauce

1 cup mayonnaise
2 tablespoons finely chopped Italian parsley
1 to 2 jalapeño chiles, seeded and finely chopped
1 small red onion, finely diced
Juice of 1 lemon
Worcestershire sauce
Hot pepper sauce
Salt

Prepare Creole Seasoning. Prepare Jalapeño Tartar Sauce and refrigerate. In a shallow glass or ceramic dish, stir together wine and mustard. Add catfish fillets and turn to coat well. Marinate 15 to 30 minutes. In a shallow bowl, stir together flour, cornstarch and 1/4 cup of the Creole Seasoning. One at a time, dip catfish fillets in flour mixture, then back into marinade, then once more into flour; set aside on a plate. In a large, deep, heavy skillet or deep-fryer, heat 2 to 3 inches of oil to 350°F (175°C). Add catfish and fry until golden-brown, 2 to 3 minutes. Drain on paper towels. Meanwhile, in a toaster or under the broiler, toast brioche until golden. Spread one side of each slice with Jalapeño Tartar Sauce. Distribute catfish on half the slices. Top with tomato, lettuce and remaining bread. Makes 4 servings.

Creole Seasoning

In a small bowl, combine all ingredients. Store in an airtight jar. Makes about 3/4 cup.

Jalapeño Tartar Sauce

In a small bowl, stir together mayonnaise, parsley, jalapeños, onion and lemon juice. Add Worcestershire sauce, hot pepper sauce and salt to taste. Cover with plastic wrap and refrigerate. Makes about 1-1/2 cups.

Barbecued Shrimp with Bell Peppers & Provolone Cheese on Cornmeal Bread

The barbecue sauce used to marinate the shrimp and sauce the sandwiches is also excellent with beef, pork, lamb, chicken or turkey. Many boutique-style bakeries offer yeast-leavened wheat loaves with some cornmeal content, which adds a sweet flavor and a pleasantly coarse texture to the bread; if you can't find such a loaf, substitute any good-quality, coarse-textured white or whole-wheat bread.

Barbecue Sauce (see below)
1-1/2 pounds large fresh shrimp, shelled, deveined and cut lengthwise in halves
8 yeast-leavened cornmeal bread slices
2 tablespoons unsalted butter, melted
2 green bell peppers, roasted, stemmed, seeded and peeled (page 2) and torn into
   1/2-inch-wide strips
1/2 pound thinly sliced provolone cheese

Barbecue Sauce

1 tablespoon corn oil
1/4 cup finely chopped red onion
1 medium-size garlic clove, finely chopped
1 cup canned tomato puree
1 tablespoon dark brown sugar
1 tablespoon molasses
1 tablespoon cider vinegar
1/4 teaspoon salt
1/4 teaspoon Liquid Smoke™
1/4 teaspoon red (cayenne) pepper
1/4 teaspoon dried leaf oregano

Prepare Barbecue Sauce. In a large bowl, toss shrimp with half the Barbecue Sauce; marinate at room temperature 15 to 30 minutes. Preheat grill or broiler until very hot. Lightly brush bread with butter and grill or broil until golden, 30 seconds to 1 minute per side. Shake marinade from shrimp and grill shrimp close to heat until seared and cooked through, about 1 minute per side. Brush remaining Barbecue Sauce on one side of each bread slice. Arrange shrimp on half the bread slices, top with peppers and drape with cheese; place under broiler just until cheese melts, about 30 seconds. Top with remaining bread and cut diagonally into halves. Makes 4 servings.

Barbecue Sauce

In a medium-size saucepan, heat oil over medium heat. Add onion and garlic and sauté until transparent, about 3 minutes. Add remaining ingredients, reduce heat and simmer, stirring frequently, until thick, 5 to 7 minutes. Let cool to room temperature before using. Makes about 1 cup.

Spinach Shrimp Sandwich

MARK SCHWARTZ, THE RHINOCEROS, DETROIT, MICHIGAN

One somewhat fanciful explanation for the seductive quality of chef Mark Schwartz's contribution may be found in the fact that his restaurant, The Rhinoceros, occupies a former bordello in Detroit's Rivertown district. I find the splash of ouzo—the Greek anise-flavored brandy—wonderfully complements the natural sweetness of the shrimp.

1 pound unsalted butter, softened
1/4 cup freshly minced garlic
2 teaspoons finely chopped Italian parsley
1 teaspoon ouzo
1 teaspoon lemon juice
2 pounds jumbo shrimp, shelled and deveined, tails removed
1-1/2 pounds spinach, thoroughly cleaned and stemmed
4 soft, fresh-baked sandwich rolls, split
2 to 3 ounces Swiss or Gruyere cheese, thinly sliced

Preheat oven to 400°F (205°C). In a small bowl, use a fork to mash together butter, garlic, parsley, ouzo and lemon juice. Bring a large skillet of water to a boil. Reduce heat to a simmer, add shrimp and poach until half-cooked, 2 minutes. Drain well, return shrimp to skillet, increase heat to medium and add butter mixture and spinach. Sauté just until spinach is cooked, about 2 minutes more. Put bottom halves of rolls on a baking sheet and top with shrimp and spinach; place cheese slices on top. Place upper halves of rolls on other side of baking sheet. Bake in oven until cheese is melted and bubbling, about 5 minutes. With a spatula, transfer sandwiches to serving plates and place upper halves of rolls on top. Makes 4 servings.

Dilled Bay Shrimp Salad on English Muffins

Tender, sweet little bay shrimp, sold already shelled and cooked in most seafood markets, are quickly tossed together with complementary ingredients to make these casual, satisfying, yet refined open-faced sandwiches. The bell pepper rings placed as an optional garnish on each muffin half make the presentation extra attractive.

1-1/4 pounds cooked bay shrimp
2 hard-boiled eggs, finely chopped
1 celery stalk, halved lengthwise, then thinly sliced crosswise
1/2 cup mayonnaise
1-1/2 tablespoons finely chopped fresh dill or 2 teaspoons dried dill weed
1 tablespoon lemon juice
Salt and white pepper
4 English muffins, split
2 tablespoons unsalted butter (optional), softened
1 large red or green bell pepper, sliced crosswise into 8 rings about 1/4 inch thick
   (optional)
8 fresh dill sprigs, for garnish (optional)
1 lemon, cut into 4 wedges

In a medium-size bowl, toss together shrimp, eggs, celery, mayonnaise, dill and lemon juice until combined. Season to taste with salt and pepper. Cover with plastic wrap and refrigerate until ready to use. Before serving, use a toaster or the broiler to toast muffin halves; butter split sides if you like. Place two halves split sides up on each serving plate, place a pepper ring, if using, on each half and mound shrimp salad in middle. Garnish with dill sprigs, if using, and serve with lemon. Makes 4 servings.

Rock Shrimp on Grilled Sourdough

HANS WIEGAND, PACIFIC GRILL, SAN FRANCISCO, CALIFORNIA

Freshness and flavor come first in the Pacific Rim cuisine of Hans Wiegand, executive chef of the excellent Pacific Grill in San Francisco's Pan Pacific Hotel. He suggests garnishing this elegant, open-faced sandwich with a slaw of finely shredded carrots, Japanese daikon and English cucumber, tossed with honey-roasted peanuts and a dressing of rice vinegar and peanut oil. The Thai fish sauce called for in the recipe is available in Asian markets and supermarket specialty food sections.

3 tablespoons plus 1 teaspoon olive oil
1 pound shelled rock shrimp
4 sourdough corn-rye bread slices
2 firm, ripe Roma tomatoes, seeded and cut into julienne strips
2 green onions, thinly sliced crosswise
1 medium-size ripe papaya, cut into 1/4-inch dice
4 teaspoons Thai fish sauce (nam pla), optional
2 teaspoons lime juice
1 teaspoon finely chopped fresh Thai or regular basil leaves
1 teaspoon finely chopped fresh cilantro leaves
1/2 teaspoon finely chopped gingerroot
1/2 teaspoon finely chopped fresh jalapeño chile
4 large radicchio leaves
12 to 16 arugula leaves

In a large nonstick skillet, heat 2 tablespoons of the olive oil over medium to high heat. Add rock shrimp and sauté just until uniformly pink and done, 2 to 3 minutes. Meanwhile, toast bread in a toaster until golden. In a medium-size bowl, toss together cooked shrimp with tomatoes, green onions, papaya, remaining olive oil, fish sauce, lime juice, basil, cilantro, gingerroot and jalapeño. On each serving plate, form a radicchio leaf into a cup on top of a slice of toasted bread; arrange arugula leaves on top. Spoon shrimp mixture into cups, letting it fall over edge onto plates. Makes 4 servings.

Griddled Crabcake Rolls with Lime-Caper Tartar Sauce

Serve these succulent burger-size crabcakes on large, soft rolls such as baps or onion rolls.

Lime-Caper Tartar Sauce (see below)
1 pound flaked crabmeat
3/4 cup mayonnaise
1/2 cup crushed saltine crackers
1 egg, lightly beaten
1/4 cup unsalted butter
2 tablespoons vegetable oil
4 freshly baked soft sandwich rolls, split
1 cup packed watercress leaves, torn into bite-size pieces

Lime-Caper Tartar Sauce

5 tablespoons mayonnaise
2 tablespoons whole small capers, drained
1 tablespoon lime juice
1/2 tablespoon finely grated lime zest

Prepare Lime-Caper Tartar Sauce. In a medium-size bowl, stir together crabmeat, mayonnaise, saltines and egg just until blended; cover with plastic wrap and refrigerate 1 hour. Preheat broiler. Form crabmeat mixture into 4 cakes, each slightly smaller than diameter of rolls. On a griddle or in a large, heavy skillet, heat 2 tablespoons butter with the oil over medium heat. When butter sizzles, add crabcakes and cook until golden-brown, 3 to 4 minutes per side. While crabcakes cook, spread split sides of rolls with remaining butter and broil until golden. Place a crabcake on bottom half of each roll. Spoon tartar sauce generously over crabcakes and top with watercress and remaining roll halves. Makes 4 servings.

Lime-Caper Tartar Sauce

In a small bowl, stir all ingredients together. Cover with plastic wrap and refrigerate until ready to use.

Open-Faced Lobster Club with Truffled Mayonnaise & Caviar

Three of life's most luxurious foods combine in these knife-and-fork sandwiches tailor-made for the most elegant of luncheons. You can poach and chill the lobster tail well in advance, slicing it just before assembling the sandwiches; or buy already-cooked lobster at a good seafood store. Truffles, though costly, go a very long way; buy the tiniest tin you can find of chopped black truffle, available in gourmet and specialty food departments, and save the remainder for elegant Sunday brunch scrambled eggs. If you really want to, splurge on one of the expensive varieties of imported sturgeon caviar, but less costly salmon caviar or golden caviar actually makes a more colorful presentation.

4 good-quality brioche or other egg bread slices
6 tablespoons mayonnaise
2 tablespoons crème fraiche or whipping cream
1 tablespoon finely chopped black truffle
1-1/4 to 1-1/2 pounds cooked and chilled lobster tails, cut crosswise into 1/2-inch-thick medallions
2 tablespoons salmon roe or golden caviar
2 tablespoons thinly shredded fresh basil leaves
1 lemon, cut into 4 wedges

In a toaster or under a broiler, toast bread until golden. In a small bowl, stir together mayonnaise, cream and truffle. Spread half the mayonnaise mixture on top of each piece of toast. Arrange lobster medallions on top, drizzle decoratively with remaining mayonnaise and garnish with salmon roe or caviar and basil. Serve with lemon wedges. Makes 4 servings.

Cajun-Style Oyster Loaves

As good an excuse as any for eating your fill of fried oysters,
these robust sandwiches are a bayou-country tradition.

3 cups yellow cornmeal
2 cups all-purpose flour
1/2 tablespoon salt
1/2 tablespoon black pepper
1 teaspoon red (cayenne) pepper
Vegetable oil for deep-frying
8 cups shucked medium-size oysters, drained (about 8 dozen)
4 large individual soft French rolls, 8 to 10 inches long
Creole Mayonnaise (page 37)
2 lemons, each cut into 4 wedges

In a large bowl, stir together cornmeal, flour, salt, pepper and cayenne. In a large, heavy skillet or deep-fryer, heat several inches of oil to 375°F (190°C) on a deep-frying thermometer. In batches that will not overcrowd skillet or fryer, dredge individual oysters in cornmeal mixture until well coated and fry until golden-brown, about 1 minute. With a wire skimmer, remove oysters and drain on paper towels; keep warm while frying remainder. With a bread knife, cut lengthwise along French rolls, splitting them open without slicing all the way through. With your fingers, pull out about a 1-inch depth of bread all along both sides of each roll. Spread inside of bread on both sides with Creole Mayonnaise. Arrange oysters in bottom halves and close tops over oysters to enclose. Cut in halves or leave whole. Serve with lemon wedges for guests to squeeze over oysters inside rolls. Makes 4 servings.

Grilled Goat Cheese & Monterey Jack Cheese with Tapenade

*One of the greatest pleasures the contemporary food movement
has bestowed upon us is the fresh, creamy goat cheese now available
in so many good delis and gourmet markets. Black-olive-and-anchovy
tapenade paste complements the cheese's natural pungency.*

8 sourdough bread slices
Tapenade (page 74)
1/2 pound Monterey Jack cheese, thinly sliced
1/2 pound fresh creamy goat cheese
1/4 cup unsalted butter, softened

Spread one side each bread slice with Tapenade. Arrange half the Monterey Jack cheese slices on top of half the bread and dot evenly with goat cheese. Top with remaining Monterey Jack cheese and bread and press down gently with your hand to seal. Heat a heavy skillet or griddle over medium heat. Spread both sides of each sandwich with butter and grill, pressing down frequently with the back of a spatula, until bread is crisp and cheese is melted, 2 to 3 minutes per side. Serve immediately, cutting sandwiches diagonally into halves. Makes 4 servings.

Crabmeat, Chile & Mango Salad Sandwiches

*The combination of mild green roasted chiles and fresh mango gives
these sandwiches a tropical flair. I prefer the mixture on thick slices
of soft, untoasted brown or egg bread, assembled just before eating.
The chiles are widely available canned and ready to use.*

1-1/4 pounds flaked cooked crabmeat
2 roasted mild green chiles, peeled, seeded and torn into 1/4-inch-wide strips
1 small to medium-size ripe mango, cut into 1/4-inch-wide strips
1/2 cup mayonnaise
2 tablespoons lime juice
1 tablespoon finely chopped fresh cilantro
Salt and white pepper
8 brown or egg bread slices
2 tablespoons unsalted butter, softened
4 butter lettuce leaves

In a medium-size bowl, toss together crabmeat, chiles, mango, mayonnaise, lime juice and cilantro. Season to taste with salt and pepper. Cover with plastic wrap and refrigerate until ready to use. Before serving, spread one side of each bread slice with butter. Top half the slices with crab salad, then lettuce and remaining bread. Cut into halves. Makes 4 servings.

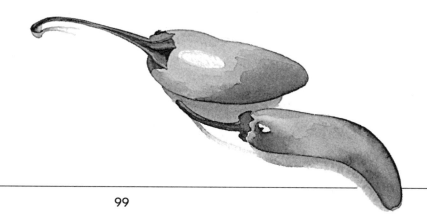

Dairy & Vegetable Sandwiches

For the most part, dairy and vegetable ingredients play supporting roles in sandwiches—the cheese on the burger, the chopped egg in the tuna salad, the ubiquitous garnishes of sliced tomatoes and lettuce leaves.

In this chapter, however, the supporting players take on starring roles. Cheese both mild and tangy melt seductively between two slices of bread in a host of grilled sandwiches. Eggs beguile when hard boiled and mixed with curry spices. And vegetables rise to the exalted status they well deserve—whether marinated and grilled or simply seasoned and piled fresh atop crusty bread.

One taste and you'll never be content again to let vegetables and cheese leave the spotlight.

Panini Tricolore

These sandwich versions of the classic Italian tricolor salad show off pure white mozzarella, bright green basil leaves and deep red tomato slices. A little olive oil moistens the bread. Make the sandwiches just minutes before serving them, to show off their fresh flavors and textures.

8 coarse country-style white or sourdough bread slices
1/4 cup olive oil
10 ounces fresh mozzarella cheese, well-drained and cut into 1/4-inch-thick slices
4 small Roma tomatoes, thinly sliced
Salt and white pepper
8 fresh basil leaves, cut crosswise into julienne strips

With a pastry brush, lightly brush one side of each bread slice with olive oil. Arrange cheese on top of the oiled side of half the slices. Top with tomato slices and season to taste with salt and pepper. Scatter basil strips over tomatoes and top with remaining bread, oiled side down. Cut into halves. Makes 4 servings.

Grilled Tricolor Sandwiches with Pesto & Sun-Dried Tomatoes

Using pesto and sun-dried tomatoes in place of basil leaves and fresh tomatoes intensifies the experience in this contemporary variation on the preceding sandwich.

Basil Pesto (see below)
8 slices sourdough bread
10 ounces mozzarella cheese, cut into 1/4-inch-thick slices
1/4 cup oil-packed sun-dried tomato pieces, well-drained and cut into 1/4-inch-wide strips
1/4 cup olive oil

Basil Pesto

1/3 cup packed fresh basil leaves
1/4 cup grated Parmesan cheese
1/4 cup pine nuts, toasted (page 3)
1/4 cup olive oil
1 medium-size garlic clove, peeled

Prepare Basil Pesto. Spread one side of each bread slice with pesto. Place half the mozzarella slices on top of pesto on half the bread slices. Scatter sun-dried tomato strips on top of cheese and top with remaining cheese and bread. Heat a heavy skillet or griddle over medium heat. Brush both sides of each sandwich with oil and grill, pressing down frequently with the back of a spatula, until bread is crisp and cheese is melted, 2 to 3 minutes per side. Serve immediately, cutting sandwiches diagonally in halves. Makes 4 servings.

Basil Pesto

Put all ingredients in a food processor fitted with the metal blade. Pulse processor a few times to coarsely chop, then run continuously, stopping several times to scrape down bowl, until pureed to a smooth paste.

Grilled Brie with Almonds

A particularly elegant variation on grilled cheese, this sandwich pairs creamy French Brie with crisply toasted almonds and the sweet, wholesome flavor of raisin pumpernickel bread. Make sure the Brie is properly ripened: smooth and creamy at the center, but still somewhat firm. Camembert may be substituted.

3/4 pound Brie cheese, room temperature
8 thin slices raisin pumpernickel bread
6 tablespoons slivered almonds, toasted
1/4 cup unsalted butter, softened

With a sharp knife, trim white rinds from Brie and discard. Spread Brie evenly on one side of each bread slice, to within 1/4 inch of edge. Scatter toasted almonds over cheese on 4 slices of bread and top with remaining slices, pressing gently but firmly with your hand to seal. Heat a heavy skillet or griddle over medium heat. Spread both sides of each sandwich with butter and grill, pressing down frequently with the back of a spatula, until bread is crisp and cheese is melted, 2 to 3 minutes per side. Serve immediately, cutting sandwiches diagonally into halves. Makes 4 servings.

Grilled Mozzarella with Roasted Peppers & Anchovies

Reminiscent of a pizza, this grilled cheese sandwich is especially good on sourdough bread. Red or yellow bell peppers, being sweeter, are preferable to green. If you don't like anchovies, leave them out.

3/4 pound mozzarella cheese, cut into 1/4-inch-thick slices
8 sourdough bread slices
12 to 16 anchovy fillets, drained
1 large red, yellow or green bell pepper, roasted, seeded and peeled (page 2) and
 torn into 1/2-inch-wide strips
1/4 cup unsalted butter, softened

Place half the mozzarella slices on half the bread slices. Neatly arrange anchovies and pepper strips on top of cheese and top with remaining cheese and bread. Heat a heavy skillet or griddle over medium heat. Spread both sides of each sandwich with butter and grill, pressing down frequently with the back of a spatula, until bread is crisp and cheese is melted, 2 to 3 minutes per side. Serve immediately, cutting sandwiches diagonally into halves. Makes 4 servings.

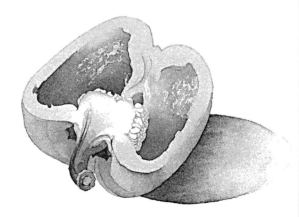

Grilled Triple-Cheese Sandwich

Three cheeses with different yet complementary properties prove that the whole is greater than the sum of its parts. Substitute whatever cheese combinations seem pleasing to you, and use whatever bread strikes your fancy.

8 rye or sourdough bread slices
1/4 cup unsalted butter, softened
1/4 pound Monterey Jack cheese, coarsely shredded
1/4 pound aged sharp Cheddar cheese, coarsely shredded
2 ounces crumbled blue cheese

Spread one side of each bread slice with butter. On unbuttered side of half the bread slices, evenly arrange Jack, Cheddar and blue cheeses; top with remaining bread, buttered sides up. Heat a heavy skillet or griddle over medium heat. Grill sandwiches, pressing down frequently with the back of a spatula, until bread is crisp and cheese is melted, 2 to 3 minutes per side. Serve immediately, cutting sandwiches into halves. Makes 4 servings.

Grilled Smoked Gouda with Grilled Eggplant

The sweet, smoky tastes of the cheese and eggplant go very well together.
If you like, add a hint of sweet-hot mustard to one side of each sandwich.
Substitute another smoked cheese if the Gouda isn't available.

4 eggplant slices, about 1/4 inch thick and 4 to 5 inches across, purple skins cut with a
   knife at 1-inch intervals
1/4 cup olive oil
3/4 pound smoked Gouda cheese, thinly sliced
8 good-quality white or sourdough bread slices
1/4 cup unsalted butter, softened

Preheat grill or broiler until very hot. Brush eggplant slices with oil and grill close to heat
until golden-brown, 1 to 2 minutes per side. Arrange half the cheese slices evenly on half
the bread slices; place eggplant on top, then remaining cheese and bread. Heat a heavy
skillet or griddle over medium heat. Spread both sides of each sandwich with butter and
grill, pressing down frequently with the back of a spatula, until bread is crisp and cheese
is melted, 2 to 3 minutes per side. Serve immediately, cutting sandwiches diagonally into
halves. Makes 4 servings.

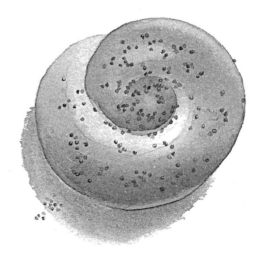

Southwestern Grilled Cheese with Mild Green & Chipotle Chiles

If you like, substitute flour tortillas for the bread to make classic quesadillas, cutting them pizza-style into 4 to 6 wedges each. The chipotle chiles are, in fact, jalapeños that have been ripened to red and smoked; you'll find them canned in gourmet or Latino markets. Though fiery, chipolte chiles have a complex and beguiling flavor, and they are worth including if you dare.

8 sourdough bread slices
1 teaspoon to 1 tablespoon finely chopped canned chipotle chiles (optional)
3/4 pound Monterey Jack cheese, thinly sliced
1/4 cup canned diced mild green chiles
1/4 cup unsalted butter, softened

Spread one side of half the bread slices to taste with chipotles, if using. Arrange half the cheese slices evenly on top of chipotles; scatter green chiles on top, then remaining cheese and bread. Heat a heavy skillet or griddle over medium heat. Spread both sides of each sandwich with butter and grill, pressing down frequently with the back of a spatula, until bread is crisp and cheese is melted, 2 to 3 minutes per side. Serve immediately, cutting sandwiches diagonally into halves. Makes 4 servings.

Fresh Creamy Goat Cheese with Sun-Dried Tomatoes

The intensely sweet and savory flavor of sun-dried tomatoes and the refreshing bitterness of arugula both highlight the fresh goat cheese's richness and tang. A good, chewy, dense-textured bread sets all three ingredients in sharp relief.

8 thin slices seedless rye bread or sourdough
1/2 pound fresh creamy goat cheese
Pepper
1/4 cup oil-packed sun-dried tomato pieces, well-drained and cut into
   1/4-inch-wide strips
1/2 cup loosely packed arugula leaves

Spread one side of each bread slice with goat cheese and season to taste with pepper. On half the slices, scatter sun-dried tomatoes over cheese; place arugula leaves on top, then remaining bread. Cut diagonally into halves. Makes 4 servings.

Fines Herbes Cream Cheese
Tea Fingers with Cucumber

*A classic teatime or light-luncheon recipe, these sandwiches
combine cream cheese, fresh garden herbs and crisp cucumber slices.
If you like, add a layer of thinly sliced smoked salmon between
the cucumber and cheese on half the bread slices.*

6 ounces cream cheese, softened
1 tablespoon finely chopped fresh chives
1 tablespoon finely chopped fresh dill
1 tablespoon finely chopped fresh Italian parsley
8 thin slices square-shaped pumpernickel, seedless rye or brown bread
4 pickling cucumbers (each about 6 inches long), well chilled and cut crosswise into
   1/4-inch-thick slices

In a medium-size bowl, use a fork to mash together cream cheese, chives, dill and parsley. Spread one side of each bread slice with cheese mixture. Neatly arrange cucumber slices in a single layer on half the bread slices, almost but not quite up to edges of slices. Top with remaining bread and press down gently with your hands to seal sandwiches. With a bread knife, carefully trim crusts from each sandwich. Cut each sandwich into 2 rectangular halves, then each half crosswise into 4 fingers. Makes 4 servings.

Curried Egg Salad with Chutney

An enticing yet mild combination of flavors, the salad mixture is also good stuffed into pita breads.

8 hard-boiled eggs, coarsely chopped
1/2 cup mayonnaise
1 tablespoon mild curry powder
1 tablespoon finely chopped fresh chives
1 tablespoon finely chopped Italian parsley
1 teaspoon sugar
Salt and white pepper
8 whole-wheat, rye or sourdough bread slices
1/4 cup unsalted butter, softened
1/2 cup sweet mango chutney or mixed fruit chutney
1 cup packed watercress leaves

In a medium-size bowl, stir together eggs, mayonnaise, curry powder, chives, parsley and sugar. With a fork, mash gently until mixture is smooth but still has some texture. Season to taste with salt and pepper. Spread one side of each bread slice with butter. If chutney has big chunks of fruit, chop them into smaller pieces with a knife; spread chutney over butter. Spread egg salad on half the bread slices; top with watercress and remaining bread. Cut into halves. Makes 4 servings.

Welsh Rarebit with Sherried Mushrooms

Sauteed mushrooms seasoned with a dash of dry sherry add extra interest to an old British favorite. If you like, you can also conceal a poached or fried egg or some crisp bacon strips underneath the cheese sauce.

2 tablespoons unsalted butter
2 tablespoons vegetable oil
1 large shallot, finely chopped
3/4 pound cultivated mushrooms, cut into 1/4-inch-thick slices
6 tablespoons dry sherry
Salt and white pepper
1 cup beer
1 garlic clove, cut in half
1 pound sharp Cheddar cheese, coarsely shredded
1 tablespoon Worcestershire sauce
1 teaspoon dry mustard powder
Dash of hot pepper sauce
8 white, whole-wheat or egg bread slices
2 tablespoons finely chopped fresh chives

Preheat broiler. In a large skillet, melt butter with oil over medium to high heat. Add shallot and sauté about 30 seconds. Increase heat to high, add mushrooms and sauté, stirring continuously, until edges are golden, about 3 minutes. Transfer mushrooms to a bowl. Add sherry to skillet, stir and scrape to dissolve pan deposits, and simmer until sherry is a syrupy glaze; pour over mushrooms, season with salt and pepper and set aside. Bring beer and garlic to a boil in a medium-size saucepan over medium heat. Remove from heat, discard garlic, add cheese and seasonings, and stir until cheese melts and mixture is smooth. Toast bread until golden. Place 2 slices on each broilerproof serving plate. Spoon mushrooms on top of toast, leaving any excess liquid in bowl. Pour melted cheese over mushrooms and bread. Broil until cheese is bubbly and golden, 2 to 3 minutes. Carefully place hot plates on larger heatproof serving plates and garnish with chives. Makes 4 servings.

Open-Faced Asparagus Fondue

*A rich and tangy cheese sauce covers crisp-tender asparagus and
toasted bread in these elegant knife-and-fork luncheon sandwiches.*

1-1/2 cups whipping cream
6 ounces Gruyere cheese, shredded
1/4 pound grated Parmesan cheese
Salt
2 pounds asparagus, trimmed to uniform 5- to 6-inch lengths
4 French or sourdough bread slices
Pepper
1 tablespoon finely chopped fresh chives

In a heavy saucepan, bring cream to a boil over high heat. Reduce heat to a simmer and
slowly sprinkle and stir in cheeses; continue simmering, stirring frequently, until sauce is
thick and creamy, about 10 minutes. Meanwhile, bring another pan of lightly salted
water to a boil. Add asparagus and cook just until crisp-tender, 1 to 2 minutes. At the
same time, toast bread until golden in a toaster or under the broiler. Place a piece of toast
on each serving plate. Drain asparagus well, pat dry with a paper towel and arrange neatly on toast. Pour hot cheese sauce over asparagus, season with pepper and garnish with
chives. Makes 4 servings.

Radicchio Sandwiches with Blue Cheese, Walnuts & Apple

DAVID JARVIS, MELANGE, NORTHFIELD, ILLINOIS

The innovative touch chef David Jarvis exercises at his Chicago-area restaurant is well apparent in these "sandwiches," which forego bread for radicchio leaves wrapped taco-style around a lively, fresh-tasting filling.

16 radicchio leaves
1 cup thick, creamy blue-cheese dressing
1/4 cup walnut halves
1 crisp apple, peel left on, cut into small dice or julienne strips
1 head chicory (curly endive), leaves separated and cut into 1-inch pieces

In each radicchio leaf, spoon 1 tablespoon dressing. Top with 3 walnut halves, 1 tablespoon apple and 3 chicory pieces. To eat, fold sides of leaves over to enclose filling. Makes 4 servings.

Bruschetta Grande

One of the most popular of Italian appetizers, bruschetta is a simple, vivid assembly of fresh tomato salad atop bite-size grilled slices of sourdough bread. In this version, larger slices are used to create generous portions suitable as a knife-and-fork main course for a light, casual summer luncheon.

2 pounds sun-ripened tomatoes, seeded, coarsely chopped
1/4 cup thinly shredded fresh basil leaves
1/4 cup finely chopped fresh Italian parsley
2 tablespoons finely chopped fresh chives
3/4 cup olive oil
1/4 cup balsamic vinegar
1/2 teaspoon salt
1 large garlic clove, crushed with a garlic press
4 large, thick slices Italian-style sourdough bread
Pepper

Preheat grill or broiler until very hot. In a medium-size bowl, toss together tomatoes, basil, parsley and chives. Drizzle with 1/2 cup oil, vinegar and salt; toss to mix well and set aside. In a small bowl, stir crushed garlic with remaining oil and brush on both sides of bread slices. Grill or broil bread until golden-brown, 1 to 2 minutes per side. Cut each slice in half and place 2 pieces on each individual serving plate. Heap tomato salad on top of bread and season to taste with pepper. Makes 4 servings.

Fresh Shiitake Mushrooms with Miso Mayonnaise

Ever more widely available stateside, fresh Japanese shiitakes are the beefsteaks of the mushroom world—wonderfully chewy and richly flavorful. They become the meat of these surprisingly robust sandwiches dressed with a mixture of mayonnaise and miso—Japanese soybean paste, found in Asian markets and in the Asian food sections of most good-size supermarkets.

1 pound shiitake mushrooms, stems trimmed and discarded
2 tablespoons peanut oil
1 tablespoon soy sauce
1 tablespoon sesame seeds
1 teaspoon hot chili oil (optional)
Pepper
8 sourdough bread slices
3 tablespoons mayonnaise
3 tablespoons yellow or red miso paste
1 cup packed watercress leaves

In a medium-size bowl, toss together shiitake mushroom caps, peanut oil, soy sauce, sesame seeds and chili oil; marinate at room temperature 15 to 30 minutes. Meanwhile, preheat grill or broiler until very hot. Season mushrooms with pepper and grill until browned and slightly crisp, 2 to 3 minutes per side. Meanwhile, toast bread in a toaster, on grill or under broiler until golden. Stir together mayonnaise and miso and spread on one side of each bread slice. Arrange mushroom caps on half the bread slices; top with watercress and remaining bread. Cut sandwiches into halves. Makes 4 servings.

Grilled Marinated Vegetables with Sun-Dried Tomato Pesto

Feel free to vary the vegetables according to what is available. I especially like these sandwiches on good, crusty multi-grain bread or on lightly toasted sourdough. Add thin slices of your favorite cheese, if you wish.

6 tablespoons olive oil
6 tablespoons balsamic vinegar
1 teaspoon dried leaf oregano
1 teaspoon dried leaf basil
2 medium-size zucchinis, cut lengthwise into 1/4-inch-thick slices
1 small eggplant, skin scored with a knife at 1-inch intervals, cut crosswise into 1/4-inch-thick slices
1 medium-size red onion, cut into 1/4-inch-thick slices
Salt and pepper
8 multi-grain bread slices
Sun-Dried Tomato Pesto (page 42)

In a measuring cup, stir together oil, vinegar, oregano and basil to make a marinade. In a medium-size bowl, toss zucchini and eggplant with 1/2 cup of marinade. In a shallow dish, arrange onion slices, keeping them intact, and drizzle evenly with remaining marinade. Leave at room temperature to marinate about 30 minutes. Meanwhile, preheat grill or broiler until very hot. Season vegetables with salt and pepper and grill until lightly charred and cooked through, 2 to 3 minutes per side. Generously spread one side of each bread slice with tomato pesto. Arrange grilled vegetables in neat layers on half the bread slices and top with remaining bread. Cut into halves or leave whole. Makes 4 servings.

Griddled Tofu Steak with Pickled Ginger Mayonnaise

*I've heard tofu—soybean curd—referred to as "edible air." But, despite
its lack of flavor in the natural state, it takes on a satisfying meatiness
when marinated and seared on a griddle or cast-iron skillet. This is a great
sandwich alternative for those who want a source of vegetable protein.*

12 to 16 ounces firm-style tofu
2 tablespoons soy sauce
1/2 tablespoon sesame oil
1 teaspoon grated gingerroot
2 tablespoons peanut oil or vegetable oil
6 tablespoons mayonnaise
2 tablespoons finely shredded Japanese-style pink pickled ginger
8 multi-grain bread slices
2 firm, ripe Roma tomatoes, cut into 1/4-inch-thick slices
1 cup packed watercress leaves

Cut tofu lengthwise into 4 equal, wide slices. Gently transfer slices to a folded kitchen towel to drain well for about 30 minutes, turning them once. In a shallow dish large enough to hold all tofu slices side by side, stir together soy sauce, sesame oil and gingerroot. Gently turn tofu in mixture and marinate at room temperature about 15 minutes. On a griddle or in a large skillet over medium heat, heat peanut or vegetable oil. Add tofu steaks and cook until golden-brown, 3 to 4 minutes per side. Meanwhile, stir together mayonnaise and pickled ginger and spread on one side of each bread slice. With a spatula, transfer tofu to half the bread slices. Top with tomato slices, watercress and remaining bread. Cut into halves. Makes 4 servings.

Index

Comparison to Metric Measure				
When You Know	Symbol	Multiply By	To Find	Symbol
teaspoons	tsp	5.0	milliliters	ml
tablespoons	tbsp	15.0	milliliters	ml
fluid ounces	fl. oz.	30.0	milliliters	ml
cups	c	0.24	liters	l
pints	pt.	0.47	liters	l
quarts	qt.	0.95	liters	l
ounces	oz.	28.0	grams	g
pounds	lb.	0.45	kilograms	kg
Fahrenheit	F	5/9 (after subtracting 32)	Celsius	C

Fahrenheit to Celsius	
F	C
200—205	95
220—225	105
245—250	120
275	135
300—305	150
325—330	165
345—350	175
370—375	190
400—405	205
425—430	220
445—450	230